Wulfing
and
Gayan S. Winter

TAROT OF LOVE

**A tarot for creative living and positive
solutions in personal relations**

Illustrated by Marcia Perry

U.S. GAMES SYSTEMS, INC.
Publishers   Stamford, CT 06902 USA

U.S. GAMES SYSTEMS, INC.
179 Ludlow Street
Stamford, CT 06902 USA

Contents

PREFACE

How I Came to the Tarot

My introduction to the tarot, this fascinating, complex, and colorful card set about the abundance of human life, about birth, destiny, and death, about hope, happiness, and conscious spirituality, occurred very early in my life.

When I was just a small child, my mother showed me how to lay the cards. For example, she held ten cards hidden in her right hand; at the same time she felt my pulse with her left hand. Through the pulse and the power of her eyes she then sent me the "hint" as to which card I should draw "blind".

"Draw the ace of hearts!" she said, and I drew. It was the ace of hearts! We probably practiced that a thousand times. Then she explained the different card-laying techniques.

We practiced interpretations and even predictions. My acutely sensitive ability to intuitively perceive card pictures, mental states, and momentary situations as a whole and to interpret them was developed and sharpened in this way for years.

In the following years, I turned intensely towards the outer world in the course of an unusual career as a model and actress. I always had "my" cards with me in order to help myself. This period was followed by: marriage in the solitude of Sicily; a spiritual quest; new experiences with gurus and life in an ashram; training in primary therapy, bioenergetics, Gestalt therapy, and meditation; and the confrontation between individual and group, between people and nature, between the soul and God.

I wrote "When the Heart Becomes Free," "The Awakening Goddess," and published *The New Priestesses.*

I was living a course in the development of consciousness. Tarot didn't seem to play a special role in it. Then, in the middle of my move from Europe to Santa Fe, amidst in the upheaval of my partnership, between trips from one workshop to the other and at the start of a new professional orientation, an Australian friend Mangla, herself a therapist and expert on the tarot, gave me an energy-filled tarot deck: the Crowley Book of Thoth Tarot deck.

I began working with cards again. Tarot gained a new meaning for me: as a fascinating medium of instant insight to be shared with people who otherwise have difficulties in dealing with emotions, partnership, family, or self-realization. I was able to combine the tarot with therapeutic work in seminars and in individual sessions. In the process, I discovered that it was possible to set many positive things in motion through the tarot—even without group dynamics or individual cathartic processes.

The moment I lay or draw the cards for myself or for someone else, I orient myself to the problem, I already "feel" inner pictures and answers. To "see" or "feel" has become second nature. Tarot cards serve as an outer picture form of inner impulses.

I have never experienced—in several thousand tarot sittings!—that the cards weren't "right." The answers are mostly very clear and obvious, even for so-called beginners.

I "read" the cards intuitively, whereas others follow the symbols, allegories, or traditional patterns of reading. For me, the tarot cards are always the "medium" that enables the insights already at hand to be grasped more clearly.

The topics of love and partnership come up in almost every tarot session; love and partnership present a central concern or problem that seems to be practically insurmountable. The question almost always "snags" here. But Wulfing and I could not find special tarot cards dealing with love and relationships. The lack inspired Wulfing to write a tarot book and to commission a tarot deck which revolve around our number one topic in life.

We are happy that Marcia Perry created the deck with us. Her translation of the developmental stages in love and partnership is vivid, intuitively sensual, creative, and powerfully symbolic. The Tarot of Love is clearly arranged, easy to understand, and positive, in keeping with the times!

We are convinced that the Tarot of Love will help many people to recognize more consciously their situation and to recognize more purposefully their opportunities for development.

If you relate to the tarot in the spirit of trust in yourself, new energies and a new awareness of life will be continually set free.

Gayan S. Winter

People and Relationships Mirrored by the Tarot

The *Tarot of Love* book does not deal primarily with colorful tarot cards, but with people and relationships. It deals with love and life, with peaks and daily events, with energies and suspense, with joy and harmony.

For some time now, Gayan and I have been holding seminars on the topics of partnership, tarot, and transformation. In these we are concerned with real people, not empty theories. We experience a light-hearted interplay of the feminine yin and the masculine yang powers—perhaps particularly since we are good friends and not intimate partners. The seminars have made increasingly clear the need for a special book that considers the manifold aspects of partnership problems. So we are pleased to be able to introduce the Tarot of Love in book form.

In the course of my first forty years or so, I had the opportunity to get to know some teachings of wisdom and to follow their guidance. At this point, a few key words on my life: yoga, seven years with a guru, work for a yoga teacher; publishing, translating, and co-authoring books on astrology and naturopathy (I published the first German book on Bach flower remedies in 1978 and wrote with Ingrid S. Kraaz *The Right Vibration Heals*); tarot, counseling, spiritual education, and many other topics. I was a producer for ARD and ZDF German television networks in the areas of politics, economics, advanced training, and culture. I gave speeches and seminars, met with people who are wise and those who are celebrities—and time and again experienced relationships. A seven-year marriage, friendships of many years, short-term acquaintances, infatuations, partnerships, disappointments, projections, expectations, work on behavior patterns—and I am now in an exciting new marriage.

What has helped in times of crisis? What uplifted me to higher levels of experience and consciousness? Where are the points of crystallization for difficulties and blocks? Which energies free us from tensions? How can we deal with them consciously?

What applies not only to me personally and privately, but also generally? What can be observed and read in a partnership—not only from the words? What is the meaning of gestures, expressions, posture, physiognomy, astrological signs, or the numerology of names?

Many systems, methods, and theories offer help in answering these questions. I have been able to establish that the tarot, when it is used in an emotionally open manner and at the same time considered undogmatically and with spiritual interest, is a direct, pictorial help in recognizing the Gordian knot in relationships and either unraveling or cutting it.

The Tarot of Love can represent a turning point in relating for every partnership. Through it we can gain impulses for creatively reviving dead (or deadening) partnerships and forming them in a new way—or resolving and dissolving them, if necessary.

How we treat our lives depends ultimately on us. The Tarot of Love does not impart any dogmas or theories, requires no belief or magical tricks, but wants to convey a very practical, reasonable impulse for a more conscious way of life.

We wish you much joy with it!

Wulfing von Rohr

1

Tarot, Energy, and Awareness of Life: Relationships in Daily Life

In a cunning way, glamorous commercials lead us to believe in an imaginary world of intact relationships between happy people—so that we buy a certain exotic-erotic scented soap or a seductive after-shave lotion and then presumably have an even more desirable effect on others. In this dream world, people incessantly smile lovingly at each other, hug each other, constantly demonstrate harmonious relationships without any sort of problem that cannot be solved by the purchase of a new detergent or a uniquely aromatic coffee. The world is good, life is full of love—with a markedly unobtrusive wedding ring on the finger.

Reality looks different. We all know that. A few unexaggerated examples from our seminars clearly show this. The names have been changed to protect privacy.

Claudia, 38, and Patrick, 41, have been married for fifteen years without any children; both are attractive and doing well financially. A happy couple out of a story book? The reality: there has been no sex in their relationship for ten years. The man with his strict religious training does not want to "dirty" or "stain" his wife, so he goes to call girls. The wife waits in the ivory tower of the "ideal marriage" in order not to lose the man.

Both develop severe neuroses, which they keep secret

1

from each other. Claudia starts to use psychoactive drugs for her depression. Patrick tries to drown his depression in alcohol. Both of them want to stay together; they still have something to say to each other.

Their first tarot reading within the scope of one of our seminars brings about a decisive breakthrough. Claudia and Patrick finally are able to admit their problems to themselves, and then talk with each other about them. In doing so, Patrick was prepared to do something which many men unfortunately are all too seldom prepared to do: actively participate in working on solutions to problems.

Emmi, 61, has been married for thirty-five years. Her two grown, unmarried daughters still live at home. She has had nothing intellectually in common with her husband for decades. Their communication is limited to the most necessary things in daily life. The husband, sixty-seven, almost always reads the newspaper at the table. Otherwise, he sits in front of the television. He is a quiet, but regular drinker. If he gets too carried away (which has recently happened more frequently), he molests his daughters in subtle ways, and Emmi feels tyrannized. They long ago stopped taking trips and vacations together.

The tarot session gives Emmi more clarity as to how she can do something meaningful and good with her time, without getting a divorce. Emmi is encouraged to take on a part-time job in order not to have to be constantly at home, especially since her husband will soon be retiring. She will finally earn some money of her own; and, above all, she will meet new people and build up her own circle of friends.

Mary Anne, 32, and Ralph, 36, have been married for nine years and have no children. Ralph has attempted to commit suicide a number of times in short succession. He constantly changes jobs and walks around with a funereal expression.

Mary Anne is very dominating and demanding on the one hand, "masked" on the other, says Ralph. As "revenge" she now and then takes a handful of light sleeping pills—allegedly to calm herself, but really to worry Ralph. Mary Anne and Ralph maintain a typical victim-culprit relationship with alternating role-playing. They are dependent on each other and in danger of becoming rigid and suffocating, in deadlocked projections.

The first session together leads them to looking each other in the eyes, talking with each other, and even touching each other, for the first time in a long time. In the time that follows they are still "going through hell barefoot," as Mary Anne says.

The individual tarot readings after about one year show a "surprising" clarification. Both naturally do not want to die. Both want mutual conscious attention. They both wanted "super sex," which is what they now have!

Alice, early 50s and artistically talented, is the mother of a grown son. Her main problems are that her husband no longer touches her—neither tenderly nor erotically; that they no longer have common interests; and that they cannot agree as to whether they should move into an old house or an expensive condominium.

Fred, 58, a successful salesman, is now at the peak of his career. From his point of view, which is confirmed by his energy and his awareness of life, Alice closes up too much emotionally and takes almost no part in his interests.

The individual tarot readings show that Fred enjoys massages, being touched tenderly, and above all sex. Alice unfortunately does not enjoy sex anymore. A mutual session, which is necessary, has not yet taken place, but a tarot reading of both partners could set things in motion, since the woman projects onto the man that which is inside of her.

Olivia, 36, married, has three sons between 14 and 17 years of age. Her husband Benno had an affair for years with his secretary, whom he took along on business trips. Olivia forced him to decide between moving out or ending the liaison. Benno tried to win time; finally he gave up the extramarital relationship. Olivia and Benno are "together" again. Their sex life has become a weapon in the fight for superiority. Benno is willing to have sex with her, but she evades him as often as possible—a revenge for former times. In retaliation, Benno refuses to communicate outside of the bed.

The tarot reading makes it clear to Olivia how they both try to manipulate each other. A solution could be that Benno first makes it clear to himself and to Olivia that he is still attached to the other woman whom he left. Olivia must then admit to herself and to Benno why she now refuses sex.

Jessica, early 20s, very young and particularly pretty, has been in love for three years with a charming young opera singer who also loves her. The cards point out a very serious physical problem with the man. After the tarot reading, Jessica says that she is on the way to the hospital for an operation. It is embarrassing for her to explain why. Her vagina is too small for his penis; it tears and bleeds every time they have sex. They had never tried using a lubricant. Jessica ultimately does not have to go to the hospital.

Helga, around 50, would like to really live again. The children have moved away from home. She cannot and does not want to go back to her old profession as a medical-technical assistant. Her husband Christopher, 62, does not understand his wife anymore and flees into a clearly psychosomatic illness. The tarot session for Helga shows her new perspectives for self-realization—in art, in travel to other cultures, in meditation. Helga realizes that any feelings of guilt would only be projections assumed from the partner who has become rigid or from the presumed judgments of the world around her. She finds new strength, which makes her a more conscious and positive partner for him as well.

Eva Maria, 27, computer engineer, cannot decide between Erik, 37, a successful bank employee, and Fabian, 31, a freelance musician. She would prefer to have both of them, but she has problems coordinating it. Additionally, she is bothered by inner doubt as to whether that could be reconciled with social mores, even if we do live differently today than in earlier times.

The tarot reading points to a third man who combines the qualities of both Erik and Fabian.

Such examples can be given almost endlessly: they come from countries like Germany, Switzerland, Austria, Italy, France, and the United States.

Problems occur not only in intimate relationships, but also in developmental processes between friends and in the family. The most difficult problems of almost all relationships can be reduced to a few common denominators.

— Very, very few people can be happy by themselves. There are many reasons for this: our fear of death and, out of that fear, the fears of illness, poverty, abandonment, amongst others—which actually reflect our fear of life. So, we prefer to be together . . . and unhappy.

— We expect that our partner will give us that which we need and would like to have: tenderness, security, status, sex, money, power, respect, and naturally, last but not least, love. The partner will not always (be able to) fill our needs and if so, only incompletely.

— We call the state of tension which then arises a "crisis" in marriage, partnership, family. Conventional ways out of the "crisis," which has often been socially conditioned, lead to abuse of illegal psychoactive drugs, alcohol, or prescription drugs, psychiatric brainwashing and feeling-washing, aggression, possibly even suicide or murder.

— We do not at all recognize our own real needs, or we do not allow ourselves to recognize them. We do not talk about them with our partner without accusations and/or an attitude of expectation. Communication is disturbed; there is nothing more to say to each other.

We are still not prepared to take on ourselves the responsibility for our own lives. We wait for a miracle, for Prince Charming (or Princess Charming) to kiss us awake and carry us off on a white Pegasus or a white cloud to the heavenly realms of ethereal, eternal romantic love and harmony.

But partnership without personal responsibility is infantile and does not work. To strive for love and harmony or to wish for it—that alone isn't enough. Love, family, partnership mean work, acknowledging imperfection and one's own responsibility.

The Tarot of Love expresses our conviction that human relationships do not always have to mean fateful entanglements or co-dependant situations; they do not always have to represent campaigns of revenge, and emotional or financial parasitism; they do not always have to play out a new variety of the victim-victimizer syndrome. Love, friendship, partnership, marriage, and family relationships do not always have to be "karmic." Partnerships do not necessarily lead to a stroke of fate or a lot in life that is hard to bear. As social beings, we inevitably come together, even without deeper metaphysical destination, to love each other, learn, grow, play, mature, and be effective together.

Some people attract each other almost magnetically and inevitably, under curious circumstances and beyond the continents. Others meet each other presumably by chance. It does not matter if love and partnership has its basis in karma, destiny, or coincidence. The fact remains: personal relationships in one form or other are for practically all of us the most decisive areas in our lives, the most important realms of experience in our existence. Precisely because of this, it is hard to understand why we often suffer most in and because of relationships, why we get stuck. And which one of us does not or has not suffered because of his or her love?

The Tarot of Love offers an effective method for bringing light into the darkness of relationships and crisis. It consists of the sensible use of the tarot in all aspects of partnership. It should tune us into a completely new approach to dealing with love and partnership.

What Is Tarot?

The origin of the tarot is disputed up to this day. Its native lands are considered to be India or Egypt. Gypsies are said to have brought the cards to Europe. The oldest authenticated tarot cards date from the Italian Renaissance and were hand-painted. Since then, many hundreds of different tarot decks for almost every taste and almost every intellectual orientation have been developed.

A traditional tarot deck consists of twenty-two "trump cards," numbered 0 through 21, which are termed "Major Arcana," and fifty-six cards which are called "Minor Arcana." *Arcanum* is the Latin word for "secret." The Minor Arcana cards are divided into four suits, each with four court cards (king, queen, prince or knight, and princess or page) and ten numbered cards (ace and 2 to 10). The four suits are traditionally swords, batons (or staves or wands), cups, and coins (or disks or pentacles). The Tarot of Love has suits of lightnings (swords), rods (wands), blossoms (cups), and nuggets (coins).

The Major Arcana depict archetypal stages of development of human existence. The Minor Arcana represent the possibilities for crystallization, change, behavior, or application, always related to the respective question and situation. The court cards of the Minor Arcana symbolize the capabilities or character traits that we have already achieved, and which distinguish us or define the way we live our lives at this time. The numbered cards point out our momentary state of mind or the influences that come from outside ourselves.

Tarot, the pictorial language of archetypes, is above all fascinating through its almost magical expressiveness. But it is the quality of the questions, the energy of the interpreter, and the receptivity of the person asking the questions that form the field of vibration for the message of the pictures and for the sincere search for help in answers emotionally and intuitively or also intellectually understandable.

The tarot deals with vibration. It deals with immediate associations of feelings, thoughts, and visions on different levels of the psyche, evoked and inspired by the signals of the tarot pictures and ideas.

Through the tarot, creative insights and impulses to live more consciously, with less problems, less suffering, more responsibility, and more love can become effective—if you are open for it!

The tarot cards symbolically stand for the essential levels, aspects, and facets of the dynamic development of the individual into a truly alive, soul-filled being who feels like an integral part of a planetary totality. We are all called on to perfect ourselves within the scope of goals attainable for us. We all can, may (and perhaps should) strive for, achieve, and experience happiness here and now.

If we are greedy for happiness—for example, through playing with the tarot cards—and run after it, we will be disappointed to look into the empty mirror of our ego. If we open ourselves to happiness—for example, through the advice and impulses in the tarot—we will find the cornucopia of our own inner abundance.

In the Tarot of Love, an entire course of life, as symbolically reflected in the tarot cards, is systematically transposed for love, marriage, friendship, and family. This is why all cards in the Tarot of Love deck refer visually and interpretively only to these areas of life and the feelings and experiences that relate to them. The *Tarot of Love* book is a specific interpretation of tarot cards in relationship to love, marriage, family, and friendship; it is useful no matter which card deck you personally use.

It is important that the energy flows at a tarot sitting, through the clearly spoken or unspoken question as well as through the willingness to be as open as possible to the cards. A part of this is in finding your "own" tarot cards, those which best correspond to your own vibrational condition, to your own energies.

Take the time to look through all the many different tarot decks. First, look at the Major Arcana cards individually and let them have their effect on you. Then sleep on your decision as to which deck to buy—maybe a hint about "your" cards will come to you in a dream. Your preference can naturally change in the course of time.

The pictures of the Tarot of Love, created by Marcia Perry, are bound neither by medieval tradition nor by allegedly secret doctrines of the occult-magical tradition. The deep-reaching developmental stages of the individual in and through partnership with other people find a modern, original, symbolic expression that is light-hearted and positive.

The Tarot of Love uncovers repressed behavior patterns, points out energy blocks, indicates karmic bonds. At the same time, it reveals the developmental potential of the relationship and the possibilities for harmonious self-realization, for yourself as well as for the relationship.

The Tarot of Love is like an alchemical catalyst. It breaks open encrusted structures and restrictive ways of thinking in a relationship. It can encourage or accelerate overdue energy processes, and help you examine and let go of phony role-playing. In short, it helps us to feel where the boundaries of the ego are and to find the opportunities for common and mutual freedom.

How and Why Does the Tarot Work?

At the start of a tarot reading or the tarot session, the cards are shuffled and then drawn. You can draw for yourself or for someone else.

Every card reflects a level of development, an emotional or soul vibration, an influence. Just like every sound has a certain quality and every color has a psychologically effective radiation, each picture releases conscious and unconscious reactions in us.

We draw a single card in a single instant. What does this card have to do with us, with our life, with our relationships right now? A lot—we have just now drawn this card and no other card for ourselves or for someone else. We focus our attention, our feelings and thoughts, the openness of our soul, our intuition here and now, on this card. Thus we look into a mirror. We accept those tarot cards which we have just picked as symbolic imagery for the current situation. In new areas of experience, which we open with our own energies, we can always recognize hidden and coded or openly represented signs, indications, and instructions for action in our daily lives.

The same thing occurs, for example, during expressive

painting, intuitive music-making, or blindfolded pottery-making. We give the impulses and vibrations in us freedom to express themselves in form and shape, in time and space. What we have created in this manner teaches us to know and love ourselves and others more.

In order to explain how and why the tarot works, we can refer to the synchronicity principle of the great psychologist, mythologist, and teacher of archetypes, C. G. Jung. The synchronicity principle says that there are not only "causal" laws of cause and effect, but also "a-causal" principles of interdependent influences.

Examples:

— Because we drink too much alcohol or eat too much meat, we become ill.
— Because we occupy ourselves with positive thoughts, we can also see the positive elements in others.

These are typical examples for "causal" connections. Because you do this, that happens.

But how are the following occurrences to be classified?

— While we are eating, a car turns the corner.
— While we read this book, the doorbell rings.

These are typical examples of "a-causal" associations and connections.

Not because we do this, that happens, but rather while we do something, something else happens.

Jung pointed out that time has its own quality. Every instant has a specific vibration to it; everything that happens in the same moment participates in this vibrational quality—it is "penetrated" or "sustained" by it. (This is one of the more convincing explanations for astrology.)

Interpreted in terms of the tarot, this means that while I concentrate on this question or that situation, this one card or that other card is drawn. I draw a certain card, not *because* I carry a certain problem around with me, but rather *while* I orient myself to the problem.

A mosaic conditioned by time occurs during a tarot reading—a question and the search for the answer through tarot are synchronized—and the topic is given the right symbolic expression at the moment. The mosaic is to be looked at, comprehended, processed, or possibly first "deciphered." We take time for the practice, and time also for consideration and examination of our own willingness to rediscover ourselves through images.

How can tarot allow for meaningful statements when in readings on the same question completely different cards will fall? You will discover it yourself. It is amazing how often similar or even identical cards are drawn. Even more important, when the readings are repeated, a meaningful interpretation of the "new" cards occurs if the person asking the questions concentrates anew and afresh on the original question with the same intensity and orientation. If s/he does not succeed in this ever-fresh openness and purpose, the reading becomes a farce.

The symbiosis, the unity between the questioner, the tarot cards, and the interpreter of the answers, is indissoluble. Dealing with the cards has always confirmed this experience.

No tarot "reading," no tarot session is an irrevocable divine verdict. Tarot is a momentary picture of energy patterns and possibilities, not an illustration of fatefully fixed courses of life. You should neither interpret the tarot cards as absolute truth nor just play with them. If you use tarot to answer a lot of useless questions just for fun, it will lose its power of expressiveness. For the same reason, you should not repeatedly lay the tarot for the same topic, but rather allow a meaningful span of time to pass before you draw the cards again, so that you can "digest" what you've learned.

The tarot is :

— a game of oracles and wisdom, a medium for gaining clarity on motives and impulses which are not yet conscious;
— a proven method for finding emotional blocks and discovering possible solutions for them;
— an opportunity for immediate understanding of the correlations and developments in life—"instant insight."

The clock does not make time, it only shows it. The Tarot of Love cannot create love or partnership, but it does show which topics, problems, and challenges are involved in a relationship and how you can find more joy in living and more happiness in love.

In the Tarot of Love all cards are interpreted on two levels:

— What does the card mean for the individual?
— What does it say about the condition and state of the partnership?

What Is Special about the Tarot of Love?

Whoever reads tarot cards for another person must be able to give a meaningful, clear, and helpful interpretation without necessarily knowing the life circumstances of the person concerned. Only then is it a real tarot card reading, and not a more or less sensitive psychological rapport or true clairvoyant abilities.

This is why we start a tarot reading most often without knowing the question and the situation involved. Tarot cards drawn in this manner result in a picture that is as free from personal prejudices as possible. We interpret special aspects in detail, using additional tarot cards drawn after the spread is complete.

The *Tarot of Love* book presents a systematic explanation and interpretation of the entire deck of tarot cards. The interpretations of each card in the Tarot of Love are interconnected with each other in such a way that you can let the cards and their pictures, symbols, colors, and numbers speak for themselves. In this manner, interpretations can develop without previous knowledge of tarot and even possibly without being influenced by the same.

That this is something special will become evident by two comparisons. When diviners or dowsers free themselves completely from personal feelings and wishes, even from the very best of motives, they will attain the most success. To be emotionally composed does not mean that one is not open for the vibrations of the tarot cards.

Astrologers have similar experiences. Their messages are most "accurate" when they can free themselves of their own preferences or dislikes in regard to certain methods, people, or social notions, and just "simply" and solely evaluate those factors the horoscope itself presents.

The Tarot of Love is so conceived that you will always receive a sensible, clear, comprehensible answer. And something else is special about it:

We have with full intent chosen a positive, constructive approach. We believe that the frequently bleak, negative, or dark magical statements of some tarot interpretations are neither correct nor helpful.

The Tarot of Love draws attention to archetypal situations, levels of development, and human symbols that are ancient and of timeless validity, but with the use of modern imagery and language. There is nothing here that you have simply to believe. There is room for your own intellectual, emotional, and spiritual associations and insights.

Opportunities and Limits

Here are the opportunities afforded by the tarot: we can admit to ourselves our unfulfilled longings, discover hidden talents, intuitively recognize our intellectual potential, identify problems, define new goals, and serenely deal with the processes of dying and becoming.

The Tarot of Love offers us a chance to look openly and consciously at our relationships, without being captive to our mental concepts, prejudices, and conventional hindrances in the ever-same, narrow track of our emotional carousel.

There are naturally limits for the tarot and therefore also for the Tarot of Love. Every tarot reading is "valid," according to the questions asked—for a limited period of time. In addition, the pictures should not be interpreted too rigidly, no matter which tarot deck you use. Tarot cards should not be misused for fortune-telling and for guessing games about the future. A "reading" represents a momentary recording of energy patterns, not a fixed and unchangeable forecast of fate.

Probably the most important limit for the tarot applies also to every type of help that people use to answer their questions about destiny. Tarot is not to replace your own alert responsibility, the inner voice, higher guidance from spiritual planes, and healthy common sense, together with your experience of life and your compassion. Instead, it must support and promote them.

2

The Major Arcana:
A Mirror of Our Personality
in Human Relationships

Based on the level of the development of our consciousness, the cards of the Major Arcana can have the effect of a mirror, an appeal, an inspiration, an omen, a warning, a road guide, a task, a challenge, or a promise. When one or more of these cards apppear in a reading, we should ask ourselves the following questions.

— In which stage of development am I in my relationship at this time? More simply: where do I stand?
— What does the relationship mean (to me)?
— What do I expect? And what will I, or can I, give?
— How do I see my partner? How does s/he see me?
— What potential for development is still in the partnership?

You will continuously notice in our book that we like to call things by name as clearly as possible. That does not mean that we are unromantic or even cynical about relationships. Quite to the contrary! According to our experience of life, there is no help in sugar-coating; help comes only in openly addressing any problem. You will also notice that we always point out constructive, life-affirming, positive approaches. Our ideal is a creative, free, and complete love or relationship that leaves room for development, responsibility, and imperfection.

Like individual people, human relationships go through definable developmental stages. A partnership has a dynamic of its own. This is in no way a truism, but a fact that unfortunately is almost always overlooked.

All great things are simple, as are the "problems" of relating in partnerships.

— Every partnership is determined by "natural laws," by human rhythms and cycles, by physical, psychic, and spiritual development processes. This is a matter of living flow, of constant change.

— However, every person carries wishes, expectations, and projections within themselves, because they are programmed, mostly unconsciously, by upbringing, culture, church, social standards, karma, fate, the unconscious mind, and other factors. These internalized programs almost always have as a goal a firmly held ideal. If the ideal cannot be upheld, then problems result in the relationship. Our expectations that other people must fulfill our own conceptions are doomed to fail, right from the start.

— Sometimes, people are drawn to each other like magic. Many think this is "love," but all too frequently it represents a symbiosis of complementing neuroses. The ego, in craving for the perfection of its ideals, hardens and overlooks or disregards natural processes. Blocks occur, all systems are on hold. Communication, sexuality, intimacy, love, consent—all die. Suffering, grief, emptiness, guilt feelings, and aggression arise.

— There are often crises in our partnerships because we have not seen or recognized their reality. Instead we try

17

to assert our conception of reality. This is hopeless from the start. Neither our personality nor the partner will follow suit for long.

— Probably the only solution is: let go! "We can't solve any problems; we can only dissolve ourselves from problems," is a wise saying. But who wants that? Who is prepared even to try out a partnership that is free and at the same time responsible? We hear some readers say: "Yes, but it isn't that easy!" Why not? We must live our lives now, ourselves, not at some time somehow later.

Without any more preliminaries, let us now simply jump into the foaming surf, the sweeping current of the most secret, exciting power that moves us in life: the personal relationship with another human being. We will first briefly describe and interpret the Major Arcana, which comprise twenty-three cards in the Tarot of Love, and their key notes on love and relationship.

Key Words for the Major Arcana

The card names in parentheses are the traditional titles of the cards.

   0 **The Fools (The Fool):** Illusions about ideal love. Irresponsibility, or achievement of truly independent love released from karmic bondage, according to the motto, "It doesn't always have to be karma to be love or to love!"

   1 **The Magician:** Beginning of a new relationship. Wanting to shape partner through male energies. Male lover, admirer.

   2 **The High Priestess:** Inner connection to spiritual sources.

Wanting to enlighten partner through feminine, yin energies. Female lover, admirer.

3 **The Mother (The Empress):** Fertile, creative partnership. Mature woman or mother. Flowing love.

4 **The Father (The Emperor):** Structured, protective partnership. Mature man, father. Love in an organized environment.

5 **The Master (The Hierophant):** Spiritual guidance in relationships. Subordinating a relationship to moral concepts determined by religious beliefs. Spiritual leadership within the relationship.

6 **The Lovers:** Awakened or experienced sexuality. Erotic attraction. New love. Decision about partnership.

7 **Companionship (The Chariot):** Specific, formalized partnership commitments require recognition of individual concerns and clear communication of personal needs and desires.

8 **Balance (Justice):** Striking a balance in the relationship. Assessment of relationship. Doing justice to oneself and partner. Possibly, judging or condemning others.

9 **The Seekers (The Hermit):** Each of us can and must have time to be alone in order to rediscover her/himself.

10 **Destiny (The Wheel of Fortune):** A new cycle starts: whoever does not go with the flow of life will be temporarily submerged in some of their old karma.

11 **Climax (Strength):** Gentle mastery of consciously experienced eroticism. Tantra. Actively and creatively living out the anima, in love and partnership. Being uplifted by the anima.

12 **Reversal (The Hanged Man):** Giving up accustomed viewpoints and habits. Conflict (involuntary?) within the partnership along with a feeling of not being on solid ground.

13 **Transformation (Death):** Dissolution of old, outdated relationship patterns. Opportunity for new beginning. Parting and quiet preparation for new encounters.

14 **Wholeness (Temperance):** Harmony of spiritual and physical energies. Yin-yang harmony in relationship. Holistic self-realization as basis for finding soul mate.

15 **Entanglement (Devil):** Checking remaining hang-ups in relationship. Neurotic attraction or karmic attachment gains influence over love or partnership. Snare of old negative behavior patterns.

16 **Lightning (The Tower):** Sudden changes in relationship which seem to be external. Compulsion to take off masks and depart from self-made emotional prison.

17 **The Star:** Hope. Harmonic vibrations from higher spheres vitalize, enrich, and deepen a relationship.

18 **The Moon:** Longing for a soul mate. Intuitive or psychic opening to new dimensions in the relationship.

19 **The Sun:** Joy in life and earthly fulfillment within partnership, experienced as supernatural grace.

20 **The Call (Judgment):** Spiritual rebirth of relationship. A call for a new direction in life. Reorientation. Evaluation of one's path in life.

21 **The World:** Completion or perfection of karmic relationship through creative enjoyment of the potential. Harmonious dissolution of relationship.

22 Soul Mates: Meeting a (the?) soul mate. Chance to decide on partnership using free will. "Joker."

Most tarot decks have nearly the same numbering of the cards. The Fool is 0, The Magician number 1, and so on up to The World, card 21. The exception is that Balance (Justice), usually number 8, is sometimes exchanged with Climax (Strength), number 11; thus in some decks Justice is number 11 and Strength is number 8.

There is a "joker" in some games, a blank, white card or "carte blanche," which indicates that the person asking the question is momentarily freed from fate to make spontaneous decisions. Card 22 Soul Mates is this card in our deck.

Which is the first card of the tarot? Card 1 The Magician? Or card 0 The Fools (The Fool)? Are we already so relaxed and composed in our relationships that we can securely stride along the tight-rope above the chasm of our lives, which are mysterious and wonderful? Can we at the same time allow our partner to choose, so that each of us goes our own way on this thin rope? Take a look at card 0. We call it The Fools. (Plural, because there are always two fools in a relationship!) Their message could be: "Trust enough to be able to let go."

The Fool is either a greenhorn, a person still in the state of innocent ignorance, one who has not yet had experience, or s/he has already freed herself or himself of all earthly doubt, apprehension, and bonds. The partnership of both fools is either still totally unlived or has been completely experienced. The Fools either are not yet subject to the laws of this world or are no longer subject to them.

We can see and interpret card 0 as following card 21 The World, that is, at the end of the cards of the Major Arcana. We start with 1, and not with 0.

Interpreting the Cards

We have chosen the following system of interpretation for each card of the Major Arcana.

Description and comparison: We briefly describe the card and point out special characteristics, comparing the Tarot of Love card to the same Major Arcana card from the Rider-Waite deck and the Crowley Book of Thoth deck.

General: We discuss the symbolic and archetypal meaning of the card, and we name exemplary people who embody the qualities of the card.

Love: This section delineates ways in which the card relates to love: in marriage, intimate partnership, life companionship. We thereby understand that each tarot card reflects the condition of a relationship and its own dynamic.

Family: We go into what the card shows for the family situation.

Partners/Friends: This section tells how the card can apply to relationships between partners and friends.

Not conscious: In conclusion, we point out the effect that the card's energies have when we are not conscious of them. This deals with the negative side of a power or with a developmental stage.

Key words: We list key words about the general and also the traditional meaning of the cards of the Major Arcana.

The Tarot of Love is valid for all tarot card decks. Thus you can apply the systematically structured interpretations to any other deck.

We do not recommend, by the way, assigning a different or opposite "reversed" meaning to a tarot card when it is uncovered or drawn upside down, and so we have not included any opposing meanings in the interpretations.

The Symbolism in the Tarot of Love

Human figures in the Tarot of Love stand either for archetypes (prototypes, examples inherited or internalized, and "memories" karmically imprinted from previous lives) or for concrete people.

Human figures of the Major Arcana mostly, not always, stand for aspects of your own personality in relation to the question or situation.

The human figures in the Minor Arcana stand for yourself or for people who relate to the question or situation.

All cards of the Tarot of Love are pictorial expressions of human relationships about which the person asking the question wants to know.

Marcia Perry has symbolized certain energies, influential factors, and developments in the trump cards.

— Hearts symbolize love.
— Cranes refer to the human soul. In Japan, cranes are regarded as the birds of love and happiness.
— Rainbows depict divine energy revitalizing us and our earth.
— Blossoms and flowers represent growth and development. Their colors and shapes point to inner motion, feelings, and sometimes sexuality.
— Waves denote continuous birth and transformation as well as the power of nature to renew itself eternally.
— The Tao symbol, the silver-gold, sometimes black-white circle, symbolizes the complementary opposites of yin and yang. Yin and yang represent male and female ener-

gies. Together, as the Tao, they create the natural, sensible balance of life in which "everything joins as one in the middle."

— The sky and its colors symbolize the vibrations of our environment as well as the soul moods or the aura of the partner.

You are well-equipped with this basic information. Now we can start on our journey through the archetypes of our souls. How do we deal with our relationships? How do we treat other people? How do we react to problems or new opportunities for development?

1 The Magician

1 The Magician

Description and comparison: In the Tarot of Love, the youthful Magician sits on the *sma*, the Egyptian symbol of unity, and tests the alchemy of yin and yang, male and female energies. Rainbow energies flow between his hands, creating the form of a lemniscate, a symbol of eternity or of a DNA double helix, balancing the forces of yin and yang.

In the Rider-Waite Tarot, the Magician stands behind a table with four symbols: cup, sword, wand, and pentacle. His right hand is raised toward heaven, his left hand points to the earth. The energies of heaven are to be transformed for use on the earth.

Some editions of the Crowley Tarot give us the choice of three Magician cards, which are called The Magus. One magician flies through the sky, similar to Hermes, messenger of

24

the gods; a second is reminiscent of an Indian god of fertility; the third is similar to a statue, with a its face masklike and its eight hands holding diverse symbols.

General: The Magician is in the process of becoming aware of his own powers. He has awakened from the "Paradise of Ignorance." He has heard the words of the snake of wisdom and is testing to see if its prompting can be converted into visible reality. He sees himself as creator of his own environment and wants to rule and use the powers seemingly at his disposal. The Magician symbolizes awakening self-awareness and the creativity with which we try to master the connection between spirit and matter. His magical-alchemical activities thereby bring about the birth of his ego-self.

The Magician is often dissatisfied with the given circumstances— he wants to explore, recognize, change the meaning of existence. He often takes chances without being aware of the risks.

The Magician works with the four elements of fire, air, water, and earth—that is, the four elemental powers—which he wants to use with the strength of his intellect according to his will. Magicians of modern times would include the practitioner of magnetotherapy Mesmer, the magician Hanussen, possibly the crafty miracle healer Rasputin, certainly Steven Spielberg the film director, the inventor Thomas Edison, and the physicist Albert Einstein. All these men have distinguished themselves through courage, originality, an open inquiring mind, creative will, and assertiveness. The less radiant side of this medal: a soul that is still "young" remains bound to its own ego, following childish behavior patterns or practicing charlatanism. Card 1 is an archetype of the beginning of "masculine" creation through "mani-pulation," literally, sleight-of-hand.

Love: The Magician represents a young, masculine power; the desire to grasp physically the varying forms of life; dealing with energies in a way that is youthful and carefree; and first experiences with and in a partnership. It is also the masculine tantric principle and joy in experimenting with sexuality—eroticism and libido seek playful expression.

If a woman draws this card for herself, she should allow herself to handle and juggle imaginary or real magic wands, golden nuggets, fiery lightning bolts, and open blossoms—she should be full of courage, love of life, and confidence.

If this card refers to a man, it is an indication of strong omnipotent impulses seeking their expression. The Magician is the awakening masculine power to balance and harmonize yin and yang energies in the eternal double helix, within the framework of real life on earth.

The cycle of every partnership is clearly set into motion by a distinct act of free will, even if we deliberately ignore this factor now and then. We are the ones who decide to manipulate with charismatic vibrations. We use eyes, voice, body language, sex appeal to do so; on higher levels, we are the ones who try to impress the partner with intellectual interests and capabilities.

The Magician in the Tarot of Love fascinates through dazzling versatility, intelligence, supposed superiority, hope-filled promises. A partnership under this image means hope for a creative relationship which brings with it self-determined human growth.

Family: The Magician interpreted for a family situation means that it is worthwhile to set definite goals and to strive to attain them together as a family. Now is the time to strengthen the powers of discernment to further the participation of the individual family members according to their personal preferences and respective talents. Which elemental energy of the symbolic tools available to our Magician suits each person best? Blossoms, lightning bolts, nuggets, or rods? That is, feelings, thoughts, material forms, or intuition?

Only when the individual family members find their own form of participation and contribute, can a common goal be achieved.

Partners/Friends: Pleasure is found in the development of new concepts and in inspired efforts to realize them successfully. The partner who is more animated in expressing himself or herself takes the lead. You want to manifest externally what you feel within yourself.

Not conscious: Male vanity. One uses and manipulates others. Overestimation of one's own powers or insights. Exaggerated, unbridled sense of self-worth. Being stuck in the desire for self-gratification.

Key words: Beginning of a new relationship. Wanting to shape the partner through male energies. Male lover, admirer.

2 The High Priestess

2 The High Priestess

Description and comparison: In the Tarot of Love, the High Priestess gives birth to herself out of her own creative powers. She looks up to the image of nature which is still whole, or whole once again. Borne by the wings of her soul, she is lifted up by the elemental source of love. She represents the earthly focus of divine rainbow energies. The mystery of becoming a human being acts through her womb, thus manifesting spirit within and through a physical body.

27

In the Rider-Waite Tarot, the High Priestess sits on a throne between a dark and a light pillar (yin and yang). On her head rests a globe in the middle of a horned crown apparently of pagan origin. Her body is hidden, but her face with open eyes is visible. She carries a cross on her breast, and holds the Torah rolled in her hand. She props one foot on the crescent moon.

The Priestess of the Crowley Tarot also sits on a throne. She raises her hands toward heaven. Her upper body is nude, but her entire form is lightly shrouded, as if veiled. There are crystals, fruit, and a white camel in the foreground.

General: The High Priestess represents the anima, the feminine energy in every person. The Magician is accordingly the animus, the masculine side. While the Magician needs the four magic symbols of blossoms or cups, nuggets or disks, lightnings or swords, and rods or wands in visible form in order to manifest, the High Priestess creates from "nothing." Out the womb of cosmic infinity, the "void," she gives birth to everything.

She is the mediator of inner wisdom and intuitive knowledge. She is a channel. However, she does not display her qualities and capabilities at the vanity fair as the Magician possibly does. Seeking souls must enter their own inner spaces on their way to her. Her inner voice can reveal spiritual clarity.

High Priestesses of a special sort were Pythia of the Oracle at Delphi and the mythic Egyptian sphinx. Whereas Pythia puzzled advice-seekers through the seeming ambiguity of her answers, the sphinx put them to the test. Whoever could not answer the sphinx's riddle was devoured by this winged lion with a woman's head and breasts. We will encounter the sphinx again in 11 Climax (Strength). Only Oedipus knew the right answer for the sphinx, because he, as is sometimes concealed in shame, "knew" his own mother both in her nature of the creator which gave birth to him and as a woman.

Pythia and the sphinx challenge people to find the existentially decisive answers in themselves. If you have read and enjoyed *The Mists of Avalon* by Marion Zimmer Bradley, you will recognize a High Priestess in Morgain, not as an entranced, already finished figure, but as a passionate woman who must love and suffer before she achieves the perfection of the High Priestess.

Card 2 is the archetype of the secret of "feminine" creativity; it is the picture of a prophetess.

Love: As a more transcendent mirror-image of the Magician, the High Priestess symbolizes the invisible, intangible, often mysteriously hidden source, the original motivations and the spiritual issues of a relationship. She represents the feminine tantric principle; union on the level of the energy body and/or on the astral level; sexuality as sacred mystery; the woman as priestess of initiation.

If drawn for a love relationship, this card points out a strong inclination for merging emotion and spirituality. The Priestess represents the power of the goddess in a partnership: the ability to tune into the sight of the deep-blue infinity of the star-studded night sky—and into the eyes of the partner; to inhale the gentle glow of the full moon—and the soul currents of the other person; to live, for once, without "logic" and "rationality."

Family: Here, the High Priestess stands for the knowing woman, the masteress, the guardian of the fire and the inner temple; for spiritual guidance through feminine wisdom; for being protected by trusting one's own intuition. The Priestess indicates the necessity of listening to and following the voice of the soul in a family matter.

Partners/Friends: In this context, the High Priestess means: openness to internal and external inspiration; being a "channel" for subtle energies; a spiritual task that unites partners/friends; the opportunity to gain the gift of insight (even into "abysses" of the soul) from an unfathomable inner source.

Not conscious: One unconsciously has the illusion of being a channel for divine, cosmic energies although the inspirations and vibration—which seem to come from "above" or "within"—represent only one's own blocks and conditioning which creep in, veiled in a sublimated form. Spirituality is used as an excuse for not dealing with the world, for escaping into a "spiritually elevated" (and overbearing) ego-self.

Key words: Inner connection to spiritual sources. Wanting to enlighten partner through feminine, yin energies. Female lover, admirer.

3 The Mother

3 The Mother

Description and comparison: In the Tarot of Love, a woman opens her arms to us; a child peeks from behind her protective skirt and a rabbit from underneath her hem. The crane of the soul turns toward the woman, as do the fish, the butterfly, and the unfolding blossoms. She stands upon the silver yin half of completeness. The sky above her is crowned by the moon's crescent; she reveals a rainbow. The sovereignty of the woman is shown by the wisely nurturing and pleasant power she exudes in her rule of nature.

In the Rider-Waite Tarot, the Empress reclines on a stone bench, supported by pillows. As symbol of her rulership, she holds a scepter. A star-crown decorates her head. Her shield shows the signature of Venus, signifying that her place is in both love and nature.

In the Crowley Tarot the woman shows her face in profile; she does not look at the observer. In the middle of her sweeping crown is a globe with a cross on it. A lotus flower in her hand shows her rulership over nature. A swan symbolizes purity and eternal life; the two griffins on her shield stand for vigilance and defensiveness. Two moons indicate her yin powers.

General: The Mother is the woman who lives completely in the world. As card 3, she holds in herself both the extraverted power of 1 The Magician and the inwardly oriented energies of 2 The High Priestess. The first earthly, "human" card, The Mother represents a woman from whom new creative energies continue to flow and by whom living forms are created.

The Mother represents the great Earth Mother, who draws on unlimited resources, representing bounteous life. She overflows with creative power. She represents spiritual and physical fertility, abundance, health, "feminine" fulfillment.

The Mother is capable of creating her own paradise on earth. Her rich Garden of Eden is not built on "masculine" thought projections or power constructions, but rather on her natural dignity and rich creativity.

The Greek goddess Demeter, "Mother Earth," is a mythical representation of the Mother. The Empress Maria Theresa of Austria with her fruitful love of life and shrewd rulership personifies aspects of the Mother, as do Venus and the Madonna.

The Tarot of Love calls this card The Mother, and not The

Empress, since not only the ruling, but also the creative power are thereby better expressed.

Love: The primordial Mother is the woman of our dreams! While the High Priestess radiates an aura that is either virginal and controlled or tantra-experienced, the Mother is sensually female. She is the adult partner of a (hopefully, just as mature) man. Her sexual energies flow freely—she is not repressed or rigid. She can give and take without feelings of guilt. This is not only allowed, but necessary. She understands how to share her fulfillment with her partner—and how to let herself be fulfilled as well.

If a man draws this card, he receives with it an indication of a well-developed anima which should be lived out in daily life. The card also points to the challenge of consciously dealing with the archetype of the primordial Mother.

Family: This card stands for the strong and loving mother; for a desire for children and motherhood; for warm-heartedness; for creative energies striving to be expressed.

In relation to a family matter, reconciliatory attitudes should be made a priority.

Partners/Friends: The Mother indicates sensitive mutual support, generous help, nurturing friendship, and an atmosphere conducive to growth and development. The Mother may also imply an inspiring muse or personify the challenge of establishing natural harmony.

Not conscious: Many people unfortunately do not (yet) admit the power and dignity of the primordial Mother and Empress because they are too stunned by the fact that feminine energies can be so strong and vibrant. Because of fear they repress the potential of this female archetype. On the other hand, there are also distorted embodiments of the Mother, people who are strongly overbearing through oppressive, exaggerated care disguised as the expression of motherly love. When the sexual components of the Empress are not (or no longer) experienced, this energy sometimes forces its own way; it then often leads to the dead-end street of a superficial, despotic nature.

Key words: Fertile, creative partnership. Mature woman or mother. Flowing love.

4 The Father

4 The Father

Description and comparison: In the Tarot of Love a good-natured, bearded man sits on a heart-shaped pedestal. His feet rest on a golden yang symbol. The planetary globe under one arm and the lightening bolt held firmly, like a scepter, in the other hand symbolize the mastery of material powers. His soul bird turns toward his "coat of arms." The card shows a positive image of the primordial, protective Father.

In the Rider-Waite Tarot, the Emperor on a throne of stone looks at us more sternly. He holds an ankh-cross in one hand, a golden ball in the other. He is wearing a knight's armor with a red coat over it and a crown on his head like that of Emperor Charlemagne. This is a typical image of masculine might.

Rendered completely in red and yellow, the elegant, crowned ruler of the Crowley Tarot looks to the side—like the Empress, a figure in profile. He holds a scepter in one hand and an imperial sphere in the other. A lamb and a shield with two griffins are at his feet, and two mountain goats are behind his sweeping, rounded throne.

General: The Father is the image of authority and experience, of competence, ordered structure, goodness, and power. His archetype stands for the protective and preserving power in the world. He imparts outer form and community principles to the internal lawfulness in the life of the people. He is sure of himself and likes to extend support to others. With the energy and strength available to him, he commands a definite effect on the world. The Father pronounces and acts as the executor of collective goals. He serves as father for a whole civilization.

Zeus, Solomon, Caesar, and Charlemagne, and also Gorbachev are among such almost unrestricted ruling fathers or super-fathers.

Instead of the usual term of Emperor, we have chosen the name Father for this card in order to emphasize more strongly the general masculine-human qualities of the figure.

Love: The primordial Father represents experienced male energies, but also the somber, looming father figure, the ruler, the older male lover of a younger woman, as well as a controlled libido. On another level, this card signifies striving for security in a love relationship.

If a man draws this card, he should consider whether he has already attained the qualities of the primordial father or ruler or if he (still) represses them or if he possibly lives them out in an oppressive manner.

If a woman draws the Father, the card indicates such a man in her life or her desire for such a man, or that she needs to live out her own inherent masculine qualities.

Family: The considerate provider endows security and assurance; the benevolent patriarch assumes responsibility for the whole family. For many women, this is the man to marry.

34

When the Father comes up in regard to a family problem, you can expect support in resolving some confusing matters.

Partners/Friends: A rich uncle, a sponsor, or an influential patron will extend help. This card may also indicate a friendship with an experienced man; mutual development within a firmly set structure; or the necessity of becoming more mature and learning social skills.

Not conscious: The negative sides of the Father include the tendency toward tyranny and abuse of power; heartlessness in the face of other people's pain and suffering while supposedly pursuing their best interests (which they view completely differently); cruelty in the name of an abstract "law." Other opinions are considered to be of little value and are suppressed.

Key words: Structured, protective partnership. Mature man, father. Love in an organized environment.

5 The Master

5 The Master

Description and comparison: True to our conviction that positive, constructive interpretations will be more useful than critical or even cynical ones, the Tarot of Love does not portray the Master as a man who issues spiritual laws or imposes dogmas. Instead, we see a person who looks upward—maybe seeking, maybe knowing. The symbols of various religions indicate that there is more than one path to truth. The search for it in the blue of the night sky is based on the red heart of human love.

In the Rider-Waite Tarot, a man clearly characterized as a pope raises his right hand in a didactic and beseeching manner. He wears the tiara, the three-fold crown, which bestows authority upon him. In his raised left hand he holds a papal cross. Two people are apparently respectfully listening to him; both stand or kneel below him.

The man called the High Priest in the Crowley Tarot has his eyes closed. He is pointing more or less downward with his hands. In his heart he carries a five-pointed star with the archetype of a newborn person. He is surrounded by the symbols and forms of wisdom and possibly led by a veiled priestess.

General: Sallie Nichols, author of *Jung and Tarot*, names this card "the Pope" and calls it "the visible countenance of God." The Master is thereby a masculine counterpart to the High Priestess. Whereas the High Priestess is the guardian of divine mysteries, the Master is active as proclaimer of divine wisdom.

The historical problem of the proclaimer of divine wisdom and bearer of the "countenance of God" is known to us from the persecution of Christians, the propagation of faith with fire and sword, the Inquisition and "witch" persecution, and theocracies. However, the intention of conveying God's laws and words to humanity certainly arose from honorable motives.

Naturally, only those persons who have already achieved their own religious inner experiences and "enlightenment" are capable of being true prophets of divine wisdom. During all ages and in all religions these prophets have been the mystics, not the theocrats and dogmatists.

Vested interests have often impeded mystics in freely proclaiming divine wisdom. Instead of the mystics, the intellectual and bloodless traditionalists and church politicians have set themselves up as disciplinarians in questions of religion and divine worship, ethics, morality, and redemption of the soul through only their God, with only their way, in only their church. To cite just one example from modern times: although it seems to be a matter of course for Christian missionaries to "convert" people in India, everything possible is done to keep some Indian gurus from going on lecture tours in the West. Do gurus endanger the Occident? Religious freedom is unfortunately often hypocrisy.

In the positive sense, the Master can be the confidant, guru, high priest, mystic, adviser, spiritual friend and teacher pointing out the spiritual direction in a partnership. On the one hand, he knows the inner secrets of the creation; on the other, he knows the human struggle in the here and now of unavoidable life circumstances. He is able to give comfort and help since he has lived through such struggles himself. He sees himself as a seeker.

This archetype is embodied by Moses, the Celtic Druid Merlin, the enigmatic Comte de Saint Germain, Jesus of Nazareth, Helen Petrovna Blavatsky, founder of the Theosophical movement, and the Greek poet and teacher Sappho.

We have chosen the term Master, instead of Pope or High Priest, to describe more modernly an archetype that we may personally encounter in everyday life. The Tarot of Love intentionally leaves the gender of the person ambiguous—the face of The Master could be that of a man or of a woman.

Love: How does a Master relate to love? Unfortunately, too often, dogmatic church masters have been anti-body and anti-life. But as much as a true Master/ess knows about the secrets of the whole creation, s/he also knows the power of sexuality, erotic energies, and the vital force of love.

A conventional priest of any sort will keep to a certain

moral code regulating social and marital life in order to "control" love. An unconventional Master may prove to be an embodiment of humanitarian insight allowing love—including its physical expression—to work as an essential contribution to growth.

When this card is drawn for a love relationship, it may reflect the desire to mold the partnership into a socially recognized structure—marriage, for example—or to live together on the basis of mutually accepted spiritual and ethical maxims.

Family: Religion creates a common center, foundation, and solidarity. Protection and guidance in life are imparted by philosophy and religious convictions. Values and feelings are shaped by accepted traditions. Family life takes on a new and deeper meaning.

Partners/Friends: In relation to partnership and friendships, the Master stands for the power of a spiritual outlook, and the meaningful application of ancient, higher wisdom to earthly life.

Not conscious: Despite the positive powers, the negative side of the Master should not be forgotten: he creates and uses spiritual anxieties to exercise power; he denounces, according to his religious affiliation, certain aspects of natural human life; he tries to justify atrocities against human life with religious dogmas. He suppresses free, uncontrolled expressions of life's joys. In doing so, he often refers to divine laws as the basis of moral constraints. It is also possible that one partner is trying to act as the "guru" of the other. The relationship is then doomed to be(come) highly neurotic.

Key words: Spiritual guidance in relationships. Subordinating a relationship to moral concepts determined by religious beliefs. Spiritual leadership within the relationship.

6 The Lovers

6 The Lovers

Description and comparison: The Tarot of Love shows a woman and a man in an intimate embrace and union—just like their souls, which are represented by the cranes on the mountain. A rainbow ribbon winds around the intertwined couple standing on yin and yang symbols that complement each other. Luxuriant nature, with waves and flowers, and a glowing heart promise—at least for this moment—complete happiness, experienced sensually as well as emotionally.

In the Rider-Waite Tarot, a nude man and woman face each other, but at a distance. They are beneath an oversized sun under which an angel, who is apparently blessing them, spreads its wings and its hands over the two people. The Biblical snake winds its way around an apple tree behind the woman, while a tree with flamelike leaves rises behind the man.

In the Crowley Tarot, a royal couple, he black and she white, in the full vestments of their dignity, are being blessed by supernatural hands. The upper body of the figure giving the blessing cannot be seen. Cupid with bow and arrow hovers above the scene. Three further couples complete the picture: a nude adult couple and a child couple, as well as a lion and an eagle which stand facing each other. In between there is a snake wrapped around a winged egg.

General: On card 6 of some tarot decks, you see a woman and a man, on others a man between two women. Often, above the group there is an angel as Cupid or as a "heavenly" factor of influence. This card is sometimes called The Lovers, or The

39

Decision.

In the Tarot of Love two people are on The Lovers. Yin and yang meet and recognize each other and can momentarily become one, at least on the physical level. The meeting is accompanied by a symbolic or real detachment from the mother and father.

The young woman and the young man, the awakening anima and the awakening animus, make the decision, more or less consciously, to be united with each other.

The archetype of The Lovers is seen in Romeo and Juliet, Tristan and Isolde (Iseult), Abelard and Heloise, Desdemona and Othello, Cleopatra and Mark Antony, Elizabeth Taylor and Richard Burton. The love between these archetypal people characteristically ends "unhappily." Why? Perhaps we will understand this in the course of our acquaintance with the Tarot of Love.

Love: The Lovers card stands for love, a love relationship, an "inevitable" magnetic attraction between partners. The ensuing encounter can span all dimensions—divine eroticism, natural sexuality, and tantric ecstasy—according to the lovers' mutual liberation and responsibility. The card of the Lovers can also represent an upcoming choice between two potential partners, or the longing for a soul mate.

A love relationship can, naturally, be a trap, when we lose ourselves in projections of an ideal partnership because we cannot cope with the reality of reciprocal blocks, conditioning, and expectations. The desire to merge, the earthly memory of an earlier divine unity, can lead to fixation within those forms of partnership that no longer allow for self-realization, true equality in unity, and a conscious exchange.

In any case, The Lovers card means that intimate encounters and "naked" openness are pending, with the hope of (re)union.

Family: In this context, The Lovers card stands for the wish to start a family, to expand the love nest into a refuge for children, to create an emotionally safe island in the raging sea of socially antagonistic and/or chaotic elemental forces. This card can also symbolize puberty, with all of its opportunities and problems.

Partners/Friends: For independent people who are not afraid of leading an unpredictable life, this card means the opportunity of having a vibrant, fascinating relationship without bonds. The Lovers can also stand for fulfillment, in a love relationship, which can be attained only by living in the here and now, not in unattainable promises of an uncertain future.

Not conscious: When we are incapable of being alone, we will use any partnership in an effort to fill our needs through our partner, even if our need is to feel needed by them. We expect our partners to fill our own expectations and are not ready or able to accept their individuality. We look for a relationship out of fear of facing life alone, seeking security in over-idealistic illusions of a perfect partnership—which can never be attained. We may shy away from a down-to-earth confrontation with the everyday problems of a relationship.

Key words: Awakened or experienced sexuality. Erotic attraction. New love. Decision about partnership.

7 Companionship

7 Companionship

Description and comparison: In the Tarot of Love, a pair of lovers move together through life in a special kind of vehicle, "Companion-ship." They are companions in heart who are drawn through this world by the cranes, the birds of their souls. The crisscrossing reins convey one aspect of the unique challenge to retain, under the more complex conditions of daily life, the union found in loving ecstasy. In contrast to traditional tarot decks, the Tarot of Love shows a man and a woman, not a young triumphant prince charging in his chariot.

In the Rider-Waite Tarot, a young man wearing a crown and glistening armor sits in a triumphal chariot under a star-spangled canopy. In front of the chariot are two sphinxes, one black and white, the other white and black, which could be the draft animals. The wagon is standing still at the moment. Castles can be seen in the background. The young man holds not the reins, but a staff.

In the Crowley Tarot, a man wearing golden armor sits in a red chariot under a blue canopy. The four animals pulling the chariot, two dark, two light, are a mixture of human beings, sphinxes, predatory animals, birds and hoofed animals. The knight holds a blue disk with a red center, which looks like a chakra (energy center).

General: The Tarot of Love shows a young woman and a young man as companions or partners in life in this "ship," which we call "Companionship." Both of them have decided to enter a common vehicle, at least for a while. Each of them holds a pair of reins in their hands. Who determines the goal, the path, the speed, and when to take breaks?

The chariot is potentially the means to success. Every real partnership is also potentially a means for both people to develop together. Necessary for this are love, will, authority, self-confidence, agreement in the spiritual direction, compatible "vibes," clear, intelligent communication and intuitive understanding, and willingness to learn with and through each other. In the tarot, the vehicle or the chariot is a symbol of an opportunity for success, for successful partnership, as well as for success on material levels.

Examples of apparently harmonious couples who are successful in a solid lifelong partnership are: George and Barbara Bush, and Juan Carlos and Sophia of Spain.

Love: Companionship indicates triumph of love. Love persists; it can dynamically overcome obstacles. The outcome of one's own initiative is success; efforts are rewarded. Male and female energies in the love relationship are equally and mutually accepted and utilized, encouraged and controlled, enjoyed and lived out. In the Tarot of Love, these motivating forces are symbolized by the cranes; in other tarot decks you will find sphinxes, lions, or horses which are black and white or blue and red.

Family: The Companionship card says that the decision to establish the partnership within a more permanent structure has already been made. The emotional forces now urge a realization of this idea. Wishes can be followed up; the partnership provides security, comfort, prestige. Companionship can also stand for a vigorous entry into marriage as well as forcefully leaving it, depending on whether the couple holding the reins steer in the same or in different directions.

Partners/Friends: Lofty plans and actions will find support.

Two people pursue the same interests. The Magician and the High Priestess, the Mother and the Father spring into the earthly arena with youthful vigor, to chase happiness in human shape and form.

Not conscious: Companionship points to some negative tendencies: assertiveness without compromise, without consideration of one's own possible losses, even on the psychic level, and without sympathy for the emotional and physical needs of the partner and others. The drive for success gains such momentum that one is prepared to do almost anything for it. Every earthly form of any idea is limited. If we are not leading a conscious life, we may be caught by surprise and be helpless if the companion-ship gets stuck in the muddy grounds of a confused relationship or when one of the forces pulling the vehicle suddenly breaks out of the paired harness to explore new shores. (Compare with card 16 Lightning.)

Key words: Specific, formalized partnership commitments require recognition of individual concerns and clear communication of personal needs and desires.

8 Balance

8 Balance

Description and comparison: The Lovers of card 6 in the Tarot of Love are shown, on 8 Balance, in the center of a red heart that rests on a violet blossom from which the yin symbol and the yang symbol hang, supported by sharply divided rainbow colors, like two scales in a balance. In the foreground, a soul bird balances on one leg in the cone of divine light. If our souls, to which we are often oblivious, are in balance, our partnership will rest on a harmonious foundation.

The Rider-Waite Tarot calls this card Justice (and numbers it 11). A queenly figure holds sword and scales, like the goddess of justice. Her glance and posture express clarity and objectivity. The red gown of the sitting guardian of justice and law indicates, however, a lack of mercy.

In the Crowley Tarot, a feminine shape all in blue, green, and gray—calming colors—supports itself on a long sword. Above her head is the fulcrum and supports of two scale pans in which the letters alpha and omega point out the beginning and the end of a cycle. The Crowley Tarot calls this card Adjustment.

Justice always means a balance, in that one tries "to do justice" to people, situations, and interests. The equilibrium required for this suits the 8 or the lemniscate, a symbol of infinity, better than the number 11 of the Rider-Waite deck.

General: Card 8 represents a new step in life. One is more mature, has become more adult, and finds oneself in the position to look back to original ideals and their realization in life up to now. Some dream have been fulfilled, others have not (yet). Others have been scattered. One takes account from the higher standpoint of the intellect. Only someone who is above it all can form a clear judgment. The value of the merits and escapades of the ego can be judged only by the soul, not by the ego. Balance appeals to reason and to the courage to come to terms with inner emptiness and the feeling that there is still "something missing." This card exemplifies the ability and skill of bearing with ambiguous situations until a "natural" solution occurs.

Confucius and Plato can certainly serve as representatives of philosophical balance. Heisenberg, as the herald of a new form of physics, made it clear that not everything can be explained. (According to Heisenberg's Uncertainty Principle, a process is influenced by observation of it. Also, one can make a statement about either the location or the speed of certain subatomic particles, but not about both.) Mahatma Gandhi was a gentle and unyielding champion of social balance.

It is noteworthy that Justice is often represented by the Lady *Justitia* with bound eyes, and a scale and a sword in her hands, while in reality there is hardly a prominent woman to be found in this role, even in the constitutional democracies throughout the world. Women are certainly the last ones to blame for this situation.

Love: The pros and cons of a relationship are being assessed. The love between two people requires some room; needs, interests, and desires must be balanced. The spiritual principles of the partnership will have to be examined.

— What energies did we bring into the relationship (cards 1 through 4)?
— What ideals (cards 5 and 6) have been decisive in the love relationship so far?
— In what direction have we tried to steer our companion-

ship (card 7)?

Short vacation trips together (without kids, in-laws, or pets) would contribute to working on and clearing up the issues.

Family: We should recognize and assume our responsibilities. We may have to cope with a change of profession. Possibly one partner who has been at home will want to take on a job (again). Children can and should carry their portion of the responsibilities, but they need more freedom to carry them out.

Balance reminds the family to stop and take the time for introspection and review of values and behavior patterns. It is time to acknowledge mutual or differing purposes and goals in life. The passage through the "emptiness" of card 9 is necessary.

Partners/Friends: In this context, the card stands for a natural balance of interests. Energies can flow freely. People come together because they think along the same lines. This requires the self-control to wait and see, to remain composed and to live without rash judgments or prejudice. The insight that we do not know anything from the viewpoint of the ego (if you do not believe this, just look at the state of partnerships and the world) helps us learn not to interfere constantly with the natural flow of life. The ultimate balance, the best decisions, come from within, by intuition, from the soul, from the self.

Not conscious: The Balance card indicates certain negative, unconscious tendencies: heartlessly "getting even" with a partner or coldly insisting on our own (self-)righteous point of view. It also shows fear of making our own decisions, and general indecisiveness.

Key words: Striking a balance in the relationship. Assessment of relationship. Doing justice to oneself and one's partner. Possibly, judging or condemning others.

9 The Seekers

9 The Seekers

Description and comparison: The Tarot of Love shows two exemplary ways of the quest of spiritualization and meditation: a "masculine" path of the hermit secluded in his cave, and a "feminine" way of opening up to the world. Both ways are legitimate, of course; mystic union with the creation by opening up to it—and to oneself in the process—is a valid form of meditation, as is searching within.

The Rider-Waite Tarot shows a dignified hermit in a long, gray, hooded cape. He holds a long yellow staff in his left hand and a glowing yellow lamp in his right hand. His head, with its flowing white beard, is bowed. He is not walking, but stands still.

You will see an older, bent man with gray hair in the Crowley Tarot. He carries in the left hand a lantern which is bright as the sun and shines like crystal. Grains of fertility lean toward him; a three-headed dog follows him. He does not stand still, but seems instead to be moving toward a snake-wrapped egg, the symbol of original unity.

General: The Tarot of Love shows two people who are each in their own way dedicated to contemplation and self- realization.

One traditional "masculine" way is to retreat into a dark solitude in order to find the light of one's own soul. Examples of this are divine worship in solidly walled temples and churches, and in mountain monasteries and jungle ashrams.

One "feminine" way, which is less recognized, leads to an opening that lets in the powers at work in the creation and from there allows a revelation of the inner being. Divine worship takes place under the open sky, in nature, as in Celtic worship.

The quest phase is necessary for human development. Only those who can draw back from everyday life for periods of time can detach themselves from confusing powers and complicated situations, at least temporarily. This occasional situation is the precondition for silently listening to the inner voice and looking upward to find inspiration and direction for a new way of life.

With card 8, balance was struck and accountability made to create a balance of the energies put into motion with 6 The Lovers and 7 Companionship. In contrast, with 9 The Seekers, an old cycle is ended and there is a search for the proper beginning of a new path. Meditation, contemplation, contact with the creative forces of nature are means by which seekers rediscover their own center. The light of life shines through our supra-personal center and flows through the people who are open to it into the world around us.

The quest is made also in order to come to grips with the void. Loving understanding and universal forgiveness characterize the attitude of a true hermit.

The frugal Diogenes in the barrel, the mystic and naturopathic healer Hildegard von Bingen, and Ramana Maharishi the Indian sage opposed to every form of missionary work, with his question "Who Am I?" all belong to the archetype of The Seekers. The psychic and social worker Brenda Dash can certainly be mentioned as a modern representative of the "feminine" way of spiritual quest. There appear to be few seeking couples who are well-known.

Love: Now is the time for a break. We should permit ourselves and our partner to take time off in the relationship, without projecting feelings of guilt. We may admit to the need for some inner and/or outer distance, to be not accountable to the partner (unlike 8 Balance), in order to find (again) our own center.

It must be possible in a sound partnership to go some distance of the way alone (all-one). Whoever or whatever belongs with us will remain with us. Whoever or whatever does not remain, apparently no longer belongs.

The Seekers may also indicate, within a profoundly spiritual love relationship where the development is harmonious and parallel, that both partners will "retreat" together and drop their everyday routines for some time in order to attain an even more harmonious soul partnership and unfold more of their inherent spiritual potential.

Family: The Seekers card conveys an ambiance of the quiet times in November and the pre-Christmas season. It symbolizes the time of Advent, of the winter solstice, an individual preparation for the search for ways to attain a deeper purpose and inner tranquility. Family members who want to develop their own personal thinking should not be hindered in doing so. One relative might be drawn to a different religious belief and life style, to meditation, to distant lands, to solitude. Let us allow this person the necessary freedom to follow his or her path.

Partners/Friends: Here, The Seekers stands for a productive matching of complementary outlooks on life; friendly mutual assistance and support within the respective stages of individual development. This card can also stand for a dissolution of outdated role-playing patterns, in addition to individuation.

Not conscious: The Seekers card warns of false isolation masquerading as an inner need for seclusion; of a standstill or even break-off of the communication which balances and shares (when 8 Balance has been misunderstood as an armistice instead of clarification and settling of issues); of an indifference in regard to present life circumstances; of retreat into oneself because of being afraid of life.

Key words: Each of us can and must have time to be alone in order to rediscover her/himself.

10 Destiny

10 Destiny

Description and comparison: Destiny or karma, regarded by some people as coincidence, brings people together and also parts them through separation or divorce, or through death. Around the six leaves of the lotus flower flourishing from a unified yin-yang, Marcia Perry has depicted the various stages of attraction, encounter, union, aversion, and separation. The cranes above the lotus fly toward each other, the couple below separate.

The Rider-Waite Tarot shows through animal symbols three stages of development along the Wheel of Fortune: the snake on the way down, the half-human, half-animal being on the way up, and the sphinx, who is on the throne at the top, but could readily fall down with the next turn of the wheel. The four symbols of the Evangelists are in the corners of the card: angel (Matthew), eagle (John), bull (Luke), and lion (Mark).

There is also a wheel called Fortune on the card 10 of the Crowley Tarot. It turns clockwise, in contrast to the two decks mentioned above. A crocodile is on its way up, a baboon is on the way down while the sphinx has already made it to the top.

General: The number 10 is an indication of a new beginning, the 1 on a higher plane. Whereas the Magician, 1, has just started to experiment with the energies available to him, Destiny, 10, shows that a special divine law affects all human actions and existence. This law is called "fate" in the Occident, the Orient names it "karma." The "wheel of life," the goddess Fortuna, and Lady Luck are other terms we may use.

Who is to decide if fate and fortune come by coincidence or if they are really attracted by our previous and current thoughts and feelings, words and deeds? We know the sayings like "an eye for an eye, a tooth for a tooth," "what you sow, you will reap," "every cause produces an effect," "birds of a feather flock together." But opposites are also supposed to attract.

We cannot and will not decide for you whether your life is determined by only yourself, by "free will," by God or a higher spiritual force, by collective and individual influences, by genetic programming, or some mixture of all of the above.

In any case, the number 10 tarot card is called Destiny. After we have retreated as Seekers, the suction tentacles of the world grab at us again. According to whether or not we have successfully anchored ourselves in our center, we will be swept upward or downward in the eternal cycle of life. New roles are given to us by the game of life: victim or victimizer, if we are still stuck in our old conditioning, observers, spectators, or simply players who enjoy the roles, knowing that the roles on this earth are only temporary.

Do we feel ourselves to be chained, ground by the millstones of inexorable fate, or crushed by the cold gears of modern society? Or have we reached the center of the wheel of fortune? Can we rest in the empty middle, the only quiet pole in the hub (in the navel of the world), untouched by the current here and now without knowing why, how, from where, to where?

Kali, the Indian primordial creatress and mother of the gods of creation, preservation, and destruction, embodies destiny as does the Roman Goddess Fortuna. The mythology of Northern Europe describes the three Nordic goddesses Urd, Werdandi, and Skuld as those women of fate who spin the life threads, weave them, and finally unravel them again.

Love: According to our predisposition, our past, and our development of consciousness, we will now harvest what we have sown in love relationships. There may be new partnership constellations. The time of using our willpower to push for something is over. We must yield to the transpersonal currents in the flow of life and cope with situations originally caused by ourselves. This requires active participation with inward detachment, whether we want it or not, no matter whether Fortuna smiles at us or whether we whine to her. The wheel of life does not allow us to withdraw from events or developments.

Nothing remains eternally as it is now. But we often do find ourselves involved in old issues and problems even with new partners. Anything can happen: falling in love again, marriage, departure, separation, reunion, happy partnership. Only those who rest in their center will truly have a choice out of their own free will. The wheel of life can represent the active quest for happiness.

Family: That which has been ushered in on an emotional level by 9 The Seekers now takes place. Finding new work, a new hobby, a new circle of friends drastically changes life. This turning point might bring about unexpected financial or other windfalls, good news, presents, and so on. Those who have adapted to the specific rhythm of life will be able to make the most of it.

Partners/Friends: The wheel of destiny works like a cosmic wheel of fortune for friends and partners. If we have set the course properly, the ever-moving train of luck can run by us, and if we are alert enough, we can jump aboard at the right moment. Destiny also points out good opportunities for working together productively and new movement in the partnership/friendship.

Not conscious: One holds "destiny" responsible for one's own hardships; the environment is unduly blamed; one dodges responsibility for growing up. The false attitude of being a helpless martyr or victim facing overwhelming forces develops out of supposed powerlessness.

Key words: A new cycle starts: whoever does not go with the flow of life will be temporarily submerged in some of their old karma.

11 Climax

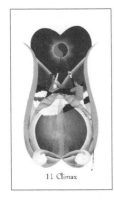

11 Climax

Description and comparison: In the Tarot of Love, the cranes carry woman and man, the outer human beings of body, mind, and intellect, upward, literally to a climax of love. Women often find it easier to attune themselves to the soul, one aspect of which is the anima. So this card depicts a woman encouraging a man to be lifted upward on the wings of the soul. "The eternal feminine draws us upward," as Goethe says in *Faust*.

This card is called Strength in the Rider-Waite Tarot, and it is given the number 8 instead of 11. A woman in white, decorated with flowers, easily and gracefully opens a lion's jaws and strokes his head. The infinity symbol above her head, the lemniscate, gives her the inner strength to do so.

In the Crowley Tarot, card 11 is named Lust. A naked woman sensually stretches out on an animal which is similar to a lion and has four human heads as well as predatory animal heads at the front and on the tail.

General: This card symbolizes the climax of taming wild powers—within us! An animal, which loves freedom, allows association with humans who are no longer afraid of the incredible power of their own natural instincts.

The most widely used tarot decks (Marseilles, Rider-Waite, Crowley) all represent this theme with a lion who is gently tamed and "broken in" by an attractive young woman. As soon as we have accepted our own inner wildness and learned to integrate and sensibly deal with our unconscious energies—with our "shadow"—the strength grows within us to deal properly with our external energies and to enjoy doing so.

This can be symbolized either by the lion as powerful ruler of the wilderness or by a king of the air and freedom, like the crane. A bird similar to the crane, the swan, served Zeus as an earthly form in which to approach lustfully the beautiful Leda. In Indian religious philosophy swans, which are called *hansas*, symbolize the soul. This is why this card of the Tarot of Love is not called Lust or Strength, but Climax. A climax can be physical and erotic as well as spiritually inspired. Artist Marcia Perry decided to emphasize the gentler aspect of card 11.

Climax is concerned with unification of our transcendent and material energies, making friends with our animalistic— anima—side. It also concerns desires that can be experienced sensually.

The goddesses Aphrodite (Venus) and Diana represent the skills of bewitching, taming, and enjoying, and the associated spiritual elevation. Sappho of Lesbos, an ancient masteress and teacher of the art of love, might well stand for the Climax or the Strength meant here, and so can the "man-eating" actress Mae West, who knew how to lead to a climax male lustfulness, from her youth to when she was past eighty years old.

The soul of the crane cannot be kept in a cage. But we can tame its natural instinct, which insists on freedom, with love. Our partnership will ripen by this. Conversely, we can best subdue the "shadow," which can also mean the soul which is for the most part unknown to us, when our partnership is strengthened.

In the sequence of the tarot cards you will come upon Climax after Destiny. Climax then depicts a stage in which our destiny has carried us upward and which we can now enjoy. The next card, Reversal, will require another, symbolically reversed attitude toward life.

Love: Climax stands for a stormy love and libido, similar to 6 The Lovers and 7 Companionship, but more sensitive, intuitive, mature, and "feminine." This card implies a sparkling, positive, and sensuous energy in regards to the erotic, exalting, and ecstatic aspects of the relationship. It also refers to experiences with partners of various age groups. Climax may also denote an intimate partnership that is at the same time joyful and profound.

Family: Climax indicates the challenge of personal growth processes. How do we deal with the "wild" energies of some family members striving for "freedom?" Will we be able to handle such situations according to our rules or are we ready to allow these energies to unfold in their own ways? In what way are such energies merely reflections of our own inner worlds? Do we first have to come to terms with ourselves before we can understand the impatient or even unruly urges of family members to surge up, up, and away?

Partners/Friends: Life is easy; we can benefit from enormous vitality if we let all energies progress and expand in their own space and according to their own rhythms. Yin and yang vibrations, feminine and masculine, belong together. If we work on ourselves and with others, we will attain worldly success and safeguard our integrity at the same time. Solutions to problems are now possible.

Not conscious: Dissipation of vital (sexual) energies is the dark side of this card—greed for even more and higher climaxes without really processing the experiences or teachings connected with them. We fail to perceive and appreciate the interdependence of energies within the human being; we feel torn in body, mind, and soul. The teaching of this card is to recognize the rhythms of life and flow with them, dance with them.

Key words: Gentle mastery of consciously experienced eroticism. Tantra. To live out actively and creatively the anima, in love and partnership. Being uplifted by the anima.

12 Reversal

12 Reversal

Description and comparison: In the Tarot of Love a person hangs—voluntarily—by one knee from a swing, suspended from rainbow ropes on tall-stemmed flowers above clear blue water, ready to dive into the depths. This person, who may just as well be a man as a woman, looks down while his or her soul bird looks up. A mirror, which shows an image of the partners still as the Lovers, also hangs upside down. Wo/Man delves into the depths of the world and of her/himself.

In the Rider-Waite Tarot, a young man with his foot in a rope hangs from a crossbeam. The Hanged Man is what he is called. His dance pose is unmistakable—it can be better seen if the card is turned upside down—and above all the brilliant yellow halo around his head as well as his facial expression give him quite a positive appearance.

The Hanged Man of the Crowley Tarot has one foot bound with a rope on an Egyptian ankh cross while the other foot and both hands are each nailed to a ball. His distorted facial expression makes him look more as if he is crucified and suffering than voluntarily undergoing a trial.

General: A person is enlightened head first. In the Tarot of Love he gently dives into the mysterious blue of his uncon-

58

scious. The ego is released—involuntarily, according to the opinion of some tarot experts. The Tarot of Love shows the person hanging head-down voluntarily, in order to look at the world the other way around for once.

Reversal shows the necessity of keeping calm, even in changeable circumstances, and of not constantly wanting to intervene with destiny and take action, also of intentionally trusting oneself to inner guidance for at least a period of time. This opening up first requires letting go. Even letting go can be practiced! To do so, one first has to take a new standpoint, try a new perspective, overcome prejudice and striving for control.

Letting yourself fall headfirst—with a safety net, so to speak, since you are held from above—is the "dress rehearsal" for card 13 Transformation (Death). An alert contact is established with the deeper levels of consciousness; you see your own partnership as in a mirror which has been turned around.

Pioneers of consciousness for 12 Reversal would be John C. Lilly (dolphin communication, samadhi tanks, the book *In the Center of the Cyclone*), Timothy Leary (researcher of consciousness-expanding drugs), and Chris Griscom (coauthor of *Time Is an Illusion* and *The Healing of Emotion*).

Love: Comparable to 9 The Seekers, 12 Reversal turns our attention to ourselves. Problems in a love relationship can often be solved only if and when we adopt a totally new point of view. A new perspective often naturally brings about some unexpected changes for both partners.

If the partnership has not been based on inner freedom, we cannot cope with this condition of total honesty and we question the value of our relationship. But assuming a new viewpoint brings the opportunity of solving psychological blocks; the reversal of our usual position works like individual therapy or a yoga posture in the upside-down position, revitalizing our relationship. Do try out a conscious reversal of the anima and animus roles, once in a while, before being forced to do so by card 16 Lightning!

Family: In relation to the family, Reversal stands for willfulness or an inner urge to look at and do everything completely differently for once. We may assume different clothing, unusual hair styles, new wallpaper—simply to try out how it is to feel, think, and act differently. We may give thought to how and why we are connected to our family, where we belong, what we want to do with this life.

Partners/Friends: More important than new plans or projects are space and time for rest and a new perspective on life. The friendship can be seen in a new way, be better understood and even more valued through unconventional attitudes and behavior. Reversal possibly means consciously keeping a certain distance from the partner for a period of time.

Not conscious: Masochism and put-on martyrdom are part of the negative side of this card. We want to be different and attract attention at all costs. We are overwhelmed by unexpected changes or challenges to our own view of the world. Resignation sets in.

Key words: Giving up accustomed viewpoints and habits. Conflict (involuntary?) within the partnership along with a feeling of not being on solid ground.

13 Transformation

13 Transformation

Description and comparison: The Tarot of Love shows death as it really is: a profound and complete transformation. The name and the illustration of card 13 clearly convey the main theme of the Tarot of Love: a constructive, positive, sensitive, symbolic, and yet "realistic" examination and explanation of the issues of life. Resting on the heart of love of oneself, the human being allows the great transformation from physical to ethereal life to happen. While the dead hull of the body remains behind, the soul rises into its own intangible realms.

The Rider-Waite Tarot shows a skeleton of death in black armor riding on a white horse. He rides across a field where a king, whose crown has fallen from his head in death, lies stretched out. The skeleton holds a black banner in its hand, along with the white lily of death. In the face of the knight of death, the bishop has lost his crosier, and woman and child kneel in fear. A sun sets or rises in the distance.

In the Crowley Tarot, a dark skeleton holding a sickle and wearing an Egyptian helmet goes as a warning through the land and an underworld filled with animals.

General: Death is first of all a transformation in the deepest and broadest sense: a change, a passage, an alteration, a "change of costume." Death is often depicted as a merciless mower or cruel reaper spreading fear and alarm. But it is really a midwife to help free the soul from its earthly body, and often enough from worldly troubles, so that it can come into a new, spiritual life. The Tarot of Love depicts the process in which consciousness detaches itself from the body. Like a bird, the soul soars up into the ether. Card 13 is then a continuation and, at the same time, reversal of card 12. In Reversal, the person looks at the world, into which s/he is literally diving, from upside down. In Transformation, the person is looking inward and her/his soul leaves the world and climbs upward. We are forced to cast off our conceptions and projections and turn to reality without rose-colored glasses. In death as a transformation, there is a great opportunity for a new beginning.

No people can be named as symbolic for death, since we all are mortal. However, the mythical phoenix, the fire bird, arises from the ashes, which seem to be its definitive death, in a most wonderful way. Applied to us that means: the ego dies, the soul never!

Love: In relation to love, Transformation stands for a parting from the old, for a possibly unwilling detachment from the past which we would still like to consider as the present. This card does not mean that a partner dies, but rather that the form of the partnership changes drastically, for example, from an erotic relationship into a platonic friendship.

We cannot remain stuck in old ego structures but have to go with the vital flow of life, sometimes without knowing to what shore it may carry us. Only when one partner makes conscious efforts to grow and the other one resists does this card possibly point toward a separation.

The positive message of this card is that we acquire new freedom to develop and realize unexplored potential, possibly, for some time, without familiar companions.

Family: An inner or outer separation has been in preparation for some time, possibly without some of the participants having been aware of it. Resistance to such natural changes would certainly cause unnecessary suffering. It is more sensible to recognize the meaning and purpose of the upcoming change, understanding that even the most radical upheaval will in the end be to the advantage of everyone concerned, if we are ready for the transformation of consciousness.

Partners/Friends: New friendships can be made only after coming to terms with those already existing. We should first examine who we are or want to become and where we are at. This card is also often drawn when the natural time span of a relationship comes to an end. Either a new form of partnership will have to be found or the present partnership will come to a stalemate or dissolution.

Not conscious: A German proverb says, "The last shirt doesn't have any pockets." We will not be able to take any material things with us from this earth. Yet we still try to hold onto our possessions—naturally in vain. We waste a good part of our lives with greed and avarice.

Applying this to relationship issues, such an attitude would be mirrored in an immature approach to life and a fearful, repressed way of interacting with other people. We hold on to our most prized possessions—our emotions—and undertake futile attempts to keep them inside. This causes "emotional constipation" and will carry the same problems over and over again into any new relationships.

Another problem is trying to hold onto someone we can never "own" anyway. In doing so we miss new opportunities for personal growth and transformation on our own.

Key words: Dissolution of old, outdated relationship patterns. Opportunity for new beginning. Parting and quiet preparation for new encounters.

14 Wholeness

14 Wholeness

Description and comparison: The next stage after the profound Transformation of card 13 is Wholeness. This is a state of natural harmony between body and soul, a conscious union between the human being and creation. In the Tarot of Love, an androgynous person and his/her soul bird walk arm-in-arm. Emotions and thoughts, transcendent and planetary energies interact with each other in a balanced manner. Blossom, nugget, rod, and lightning, as well as the complete Tao, suggest the presence of all four vital elements complementing each other to form a whole.

In the Rider-Waite Tarot, a winged angelic being with a radiant halo around its head pours the water of life from one goblet into the other. The natural elements of water, earth, fire (represented here as the sun), and air form the surroundings—the angel has returned to the earth right after "death." A triangle like a pyramid on its heart center suggests that an initiation has taken place.

In the Crowley Tarot, a double-faced woman stands before a sun corona and under two thin crescent moons. She pours water and fire into an alchemist's kettle, which hangs above a fire. A white lion and a red eagle appear to be feasting on the bubbling contents of this cauldron.

We call this card Wholeness; Waite gives it the name Temperance; Crowley calls it Art.

General: When the ego dies and the soul is resurrected we gain new dimensions of life. Seemingly irreconcilable opposites melt together in a virtually alchemical process. A new balance can be achieved not only in ourselves, but also through us in our environment!

The angelic form connects heavenly and earthly elements and imparts invigorating supernatural powers to the earth: the water of life in the Marseilles and Rider-Waite tarots, water and fire in the Crowley Tarot, the rainbow light with all of life's colors in the Tarot of Love. Yin and yang, feminine and masculine powers, spiritual and physical values and experiences are in harmony with each other. Partnership can be experienced on a new, higher level.

There are no famous examples for Wholeness in the realm of partnership, perhaps because relationships, particularly those of celebrities, are without moderation. But we do find in other areas of life examples of Wholeness actualized. Johann Sebastian Bach is an example in the area of music as he proclaims the heavenly order, which is to be striven for here on earth, with exalted clarity; Wolfgang Amadeus Mozart inspires sensitive people to experience heaven here on earth. Leonardo da Vinci depicted the inherent harmony of human dimensions; the (androgynous?) Mona Lisa is evidence of this. Prince Gautama, who became Buddha and established the measure of the middle path, is the criterion of a complete life.

Love: This card indicates that the masculine and feminine energies in a relationship have been balanced—or that we face the challenge to learn to balance them. Fulfillment through the sophisticated art of love, like tantra—physically sensual, emotionally affectionate, and spiritually uplifting— can be a good help and a stimulating approach.

Those who are without a partner when they draw this card are given a cue to make up their minds as to which type of partner they want to attract. It is our own degree of wholeness and our own aura that actually determine who enters our life.

Family: In terms of the family, Wholeness symbolizes a growing mutual understanding and tolerance for the individuality of various family members. Processes of growth can be worked on and/or completed without too much psychological stress.

Partners/Friends: You understand and complement each other in a creative manner. This generates a new energy that is both prolific and gentle. Possibly for the first time in your life you may encounter a soul mate or recognize someone from your existing circle of friends to be just that.

Not conscious: Wholeness warns against wasting or dissipating energies. Good opportunities to use subtle energies may not be perceived. They may be blocked instead by old behavior patterns. One typical example in love relationships: one partner, usually the man, does not appreciate the other's emotional needs and the opportunity for enticing playfulness on many levels of a loving exchange, but just wants to "go for it" right away.

If the magnificent possibilities to be harmoniously creative are squandered, Entanglement, card 15, is waiting for us.

Key words: Balancing of spiritual and physical energies. Yin-yang harmony in the partnership. Basis for a partnership with the soul mate through holistic experience of the self.

15 Entanglement

15 Entanglement

Description and comparison: We see only two legs and two arms on card 15 in the Tarot of Love. These are obviously people holding onto each other with their arms while at the same time trying to disengage themselves from each other by breaking away with their legs. A snake, symbol of both seduction and wisdom, winds around the two legs and emphasizes their indecisiveness and entanglement, attraction and repulsion—a modern term for this syndrome is co-dependency. The creeping plants also underline this. The one visible soul bird flies as if it would crash at any moment. The red heart is broken in two halves, flames lick around the separated yin and yang symbols.

In the Rider-Waite Tarot, an ugly devil rules over a block to which two naked people—a man and a woman—are chained. Both people wear the horns and tail of the devil. While the devil further ignites the man's flaming tail, grapes sprout from the tail of the woman.

In the Crowley Tarot, an almost impish-looking billy goat with massive horns grins in the underworld. He stands in front of something that looks like an erect penis whose tip disappears somewhere in the world beyond. The transparent testicles are populated by bluish-colored people whose activities are clearly of a lustful nature.

General: In the common vernacular in Germany there are "Death and Devil," the two villains and scapegoats of the (unconscious) people. The "Devil" is the lie most frequently used to frighten people; according to this lie, a supposedly diabolical power outside of us tempts us and leads us to ruin.

67

This energy must also appear as one of the archetypes in the tarot.

But do not let yourself be fooled. The Devil is at worst a reflection of our own imagination, illusions, fears, and desires, of our lust which has been repressed, suppressed, or perverted since it has not been lived out, and of our unrecognized, unmastered shadow side. If we do not voluntarily grapple with it, we will be forced to surrender to the shadow we ourselves have created. The usual tarot systems present the Devil as a demigod, a goat-headed creature who chains two humans. The Tarot of Love purposely parts from this misleading portrayal. Instead, we see two people whose legs are going in opposite directions while they still hold each other by the arms and are not about to let go: a classic case of Entanglement. We place more value on the aspect of the "Devil" that embodies a struggle between union and separation than on the perspective that we are first tempted and then bound by dark powers.

People in history such as Hitler and Stalin, and perhaps Genghis Khan and Napoleon, stand for the uncontrolled "devilish" aspect. However, it should not be overlooked that they could act so devilishly only with the tacit consent of their collective of people. We are all somehow entangled in the deeds of such people. We support or tolerate or repress our feelings about them, we do not talk about them, and we look away from them. Possibly even our own negative thoughts initially make such phenomena possible.

Love: Attraction always precedes entanglement. The most "devilish" characteristic of a one-sided or mutual entanglement is that the co-dependency goes unnoticed. We may think of it as love or consideration or assuming responsibility for the other person. We want the partner to play a role for us and with us which does not reflect reality. We see what we want to see in the other person, not how we and the partner really are. If the attraction is primarily sexual, our inner anxieties and outer conflicts will have no end—until the Lightning of card 16 strikes. Sexual dependence/co-dependence is one aspect of Entanglement.

When we draw this card in a tarot reading, we are challenged to probe the basement of our psyche and the attic of our idealism for contradictory emotional impulses and unclear feelings between "blind love" and "blind hate," which only lead us deeper into suffering.

Entanglement represents the urgency of a decision between true love and ego trips. It presents a great opportunity to find out who holds on to whom and why.

Family: Within the family, apart from pointing out potential co-dependencies, Entanglement stands for the tendency to condemn behavior deviating from set rules; for example, the daughter brings home an "unacceptable" new date or the son hangs out at the "wrong" places. Entanglement also stands for the common inclination of insecure or lonely parents to restrain the children's progress on their own chosen paths, often under the guise of parental care.

If you draw this card, you are called on to share honestly the motivations of your own desires and behavior with your family—and they with you. A desire for freedom naturally does not legitimize irresponsible actions.

Partners/Friends: This card shows the tendency to hold another person emotionally captive. Sometimes Entanglement hints at gradually growing mistrust between friends who do not muster the "courage" to talk openly about problems. So Entanglement calls on us to clear up problems, check on partnerships that have been outlived and reshape them where needed.

Not conscious: If we draw this card and feel that our life or the specific situation we are asking about does not need any change, then we are obviously sticking our heads into the sand like an ostrich or are already in very murky waters and do not even know it. Life will bring about the consequences we have provoked. (See card 16 Lightning.) Entanglement may also imply that we are being exploited and/or controlled (emotionally, physically, financially, and so on) without being aware of it or admitting it to ourselves. If so, we should seek help.

Key words: Checking remaining hang-ups in relationship. Neurotic attraction or karmic attachment gains influence over love or partnership. Snare of old negative behavior patterns.

16 Lightning

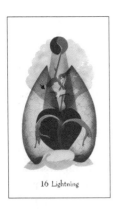

16 Lightning

Description and comparison: The monadic egg of primordial unity is struck by lightning, not out of the blue but coming down from the Tao of perfect union between yin and yang. The cracking egg sets free two soul birds as the outer beings dive downward into the cool reality of their subconscious and unconscious dimensions, which they now immediately experience.

A flash of lightning in the pitch-black sky strikes the top of a prison tower in the Rider-Waite Tarot. Fire breaks out of the windows and two formerly noble figures fall terrified into uncertainty.

Flames blazing out of a mouth make a building collapse

70

in the Crowley Tarot. Cubistic beings, perhaps humans, fly through the air as will-less as dolls. A large eye above the scene radiates energy into every last corner of it. A peace dove and radiant dragon add something conciliatory to the picture which is in black, red, and dirty yellow.

General: Lightning strikes, old structures are destroyed. Even if we built these solid structures as protection, they have turned into a prison for us. Since we usually do not willingly leave self-built prisons, lightning must strike. The lightning then means that we are freed!

The Tarot of Love calls this card Lightning; in other tarot systems it is The Tower, The Tower of Destruction, or The House of God. On all of the cards, lightning plays the most important role, for it is lightning alone, coming unexpectedly, that has the power to burst our shackles and chains of entanglement.

If we do not want to grapple with the shadow of our own "devil," a merciful destiny sends lightning to us. Lightning then stands for radical change, which appears to be destructive and is externally forced on us against our will. In reality, only the elemental power of lightning can finally break apart all the emotional blocks, prejudices, dogmas, concepts, masks, and projections which have hardened into rigid shells.

We must find the way of life and travel it, instead of trying to force life to follow our will and our ideas. Our ego trips build the prison walls around us—walls that can be destroyed only by "violence." The power of lightning seems to be destructive and painful, but in reality, the violent bolt is our last salvation and the help that enables us to survive.

The elemental power of lightning, which strikes down from higher spheres in order to destroy the old and create space for the new to live, is personified by the examples of Joan of Arc, who paid with her life for her convictions, George

Washington, Lenin, Mao, and Osho Rajneesh (formerly called Bhagwan), who left no single outdated social, political, psychological, or spiritual behavior pattern untouched.

Love: Our ego is deposed, our masks torn off. It does not matter if we do or do not like what we see. For a love relationship, Lightning signifies a stormy period during which external events and occurrences appear to shake up completely the partnership. In reality, the shakeup is not a result of outer circumstances but rather the natural effect of our own previous thoughts, feelings, and deeds. We feel ourselves to be naked in front of each other—inviting new energies to emerge. Life presents us with a new beginning, even if we did not voluntarily opt for it. (Card 17 The Star follows this up.)

Lightning also exemplifies a time during which we may not (or no longer) be able to give as much as we wish or are accustomed to give because so much is happening "to" us.

Family: Chains of outlived habits, forged by guilt, fear, and power play, are being crushed. No stone is left standing. This could mean a departure from a housing arrangement where the family lived together under one roof. As devastating as Lightning might seem at first, it always provides a liberating new beginning, which we would otherwise have avoided.

Partners/Friends: Intense clashes purify the partnership like a violent thunderstorm. Hardened positions and false claims to authority come under fire. In friendships there are kill-or-cure remedies for controversies.

Not conscious: If we have been dozing through our life instead of intently facing the vital challenges, we might experience the lightning bolt—the shock remedy or medicine of destiny's choice—as such a crushing force that we physically break down. We should recognize in due time that everything

72

within ourselves that we do not cope with now will one day take on physical form to challenge us as an "external" force. So Lightning tells us that it is the eleventh hour, time to assume responsibility for our life and our destiny.

Key words: Sudden changes in relationship which seem to be external. Compulsion to take off masks and leave self-made emotional prison.

17 The Star

17 The Star

Description and comparison: Soft rainbow light pours down from a centered star in the Tarot of Love. A couple, tenderly holding each other and a cornucopia richly filled with the pure gifts of nature, gaze up into the sky. The cranes also look up at the starry heavens.

In the Rider-Waite deck, under a large yellow star and seven smaller white stars in the light-blue sky, a nude woman kneels next to a pond and pours out two jugs of water. She empties one of the jugs into the water itself, the other onto the greening earth next to it. This female form is reminiscent of the figure on card 14 Temperance.

A nude woman also appears in the Crowley Tarot. In front of a transparent giant globe and under a star turning in spirals, she pours liquid energy onto herself from a greenish bowl in her right hand; at the same time, she lets the same energy flow to the earth from a bluish bowl in her left hand.

General: The heavens again open up in the Star, not to throw us down with a lightning bolt, but rather to shower us with gifts. The Star stands for a ray of hope which animates not only us but also pours through us into our environment as if from a cornucopia or like the water of life. We become the recipients of these higher gifts and should become mediators for them. The Star also represents the first fruitful contact with the so-called "higher self."

The founder of the Red Cross, Jean Henri Dunant, the Sufi saint Mira Bai, and certainly the nymphs of Greek myth belong to those who have turned their sensual and artistic inspirations into loving creative activities for their environment.

Love: After stormy times in the relationship, the Star promises new hope for a more calm and soothing life. There comes a veritable springtime of the heart—new emotional sharing and caring, an inspired chance for falling in love again. Harmonious energies flow between all centers (chakras) in people, and we are able to transmit energies to others in a very beneficial way. New hopes arise for life and love. The Star signifies a good time to become pregnant.

Family: After a family "catastrophe," you will be able to communicate on higher levels of understanding with more loving consideration. It is a good time to look for new goals and to work on them with other members of the family. The Star also shows renewed enjoyment of family life and common activities.

Partners/Friends: There is an intuitive harmony in how partners and friends work or live together. They externally achieve what they have been inwardly guided to do. New trust is created. Additionally, The Star shows openness for spiritual or mental stimulation and socially or culturally constructive activities.

Not conscious: One misses out on great opportunities for fun in personal growth because one remains stuck in mourning for past fantasies. Whoever misses this chance for a new beginning will still feel good in the time of the Star—yet they will miss out on the sparkle of an elusive shooting star.

Key words: Hope. Harmonic vibrations from higher spheres vitalize, enrich, and deepen a relationship.

18 The Moon

18 The Moon

Description and comparison: A nude couple sit back to back on a heart rising out of blue waters, wrapped in the light of a soft rainbow beam which pours down some of the mysterious powers of the silvery moon above. While the two cranes are already soaring up to the promising moon, the couple seem to be dreamily engulfed in the image of the moon reflected by the water.

In the Rider-Waite Tarot, a crab leaves its ancestral waters and follows the sandy path toward the moon in the distance, apparently magically attracted by its beams. The way leads between two dogs and two (watch?) towers out into a strange mountain world. As if in encouragement, the moon rains down a sort of manna.

We find a design similar to the Rider-Waite Tarot in Crowley's deck. An Egyptian scarab, in the place of the crab, pushes a golden ball in front of itself. With this ball, the scarab must make its way between two Egyptian creatures which look as if they came from the underworld. It must pass from a world of light through a dark one to get into the light again.

General: The Moon challenges us before it gives us anything.

While the Star gives without question, the Moon first reflects the state of our soul, which determines what we will receive. Our longings for another reality in life, for the realization of dreams and visions, are sparked by the Moon. But the Moon lets us enter its mysterious wonderland only after we have passed difficult trials. The core of these tests is always that we must decide whether we want to entrust our path in life to the logical, rational intellect or have more trust in the silent voice of our intuition. Through such tests, we find our individual path that leads to true fulfillment. Only if we are prepared should we start out on this path.

Figures symbolic of the Moon are the Egyptian goddess Isis, Mother Mary, who is beyond church dogma, and possibly the mysterious Greek prophet Cassandra, who foresaw the fall of Troy.

In German the moon is masculine (*der Mond*) and the sun is feminine (*die Sonne*); in the Romance languages, French for example, the moon is feminine (*la lune*) and the sun is masculine (*le soleil*). According to the Germanic origins, the sun is the primordial mother and the moon a masculine reflection of this feminine creative power.

Love: The longing for a deep love, which has been only a dream, is symbolized by the Moon. Idealistic projections of love relationships arise from the unconscious or from memories of earlier lives. This is a chance to experience magical energies within the partnership, even if we only vaguely sense these energies and do not consciously grasp them. We are challenged to continue together the path of life on which we have already started, and to be open to a profound transformation, deepening, and search in the partnership. Moon times are full of magic.

Family: The previous family situation loses impact. We see the family as if through other eyes. Visions and hopes of true community take the place of habitual role-playing and polite masking of real feelings. We try to find a more direct communication and connection with other members of the family on higher levels than usual because we become more aware of our distinctions.

Partners/Friends: Two seekers who have been groping on their own long enough in the darkness of earthly existence have found each other and now discover similarities in their respective fates. Both have a premonition of a home which is not of this world. They have not yet gone the path leading there, but both are prepared to travel together some distance toward the mystery.

Not conscious: If we do not live a conscious life, the powers of the moon lead us to lose ourselves in illusions and irrational anxieties, or to let ourselves be ruled by supernatural impulses. It is well documented that the times of full moon and new moon are times of crises; more accidents, homicides, suicides, and complications during surgery occur then than at any other time.

Key words: Longing for a soul mate. Intuitive or psychic opening to new dimensions in the relationship.

19 The Sun

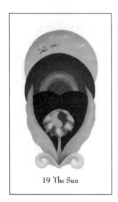

19 The Sun

Description and comparison: The violet blossom of longing has opened fully with the symbol of the Tao. A family dances on the red heart of love, in front of the golden sun and beneath a rainbow. Four soul birds rise in the distant blue of the wide sky, flying toward an unknown destination.

In the Rider-Waite Tarot, an oversized sun warms with its rays a small, naked child who joyfully rides on a young white horse in front of a wall lined with blossoming sunflowers. The child holds an orange scarf that cheerfully flutters in the wind.

As in most other tarot decks, the Crowley Tarot shows two naked children on card 19. On butterfly wings they hover in front of a green hill under a circle of sunlight, the rays of which mark the twelve positions of the zodiac.

General: The Sun represents paradise on earth, a condition that resembles the Garden of Eden, within the limitations of our planet Earth and our dimensions of body, space, and time. Life can be taken and enjoyed as it comes, as it is, and also as it passes again!

Childish joy of life, confidence, worldly success, pleasure, creative energy, warm-hearted humanity, and exuberant power characterize this sun period. The Sun means happiness!

The Egyptian sun god Ra represents this tarot card as does the emperor Charles V, in whose realm the sun never set. The French Sun King Louis XIV is another sun figure. The Austrian empress Maria Theresa (who also appeared as a

Mother figure) ruled a huge kingdom; her silver *thaler* was accepted almost universally as payment and is still accepted today in some Arab countries. She did not avoid conflicts of war if they were necessary. Although she was a loving wife to her husband and bore no less than sixteen children, she also had lovers on the side since her spouse did not seem to meet all of her demands.

Love: We can finally draw on unlimited resources and delve right into the richness of life, if we are ready to appreciate properly our potential and exercise it fully. At this stage of our life's journey, we may want to grant ourselves a wonderful stay at an elegant luxury hotel or on a lonely romantic island—with a radiant, treasured beloved at our side.

The Sun represents happy and healthy personal growth and a colorfully varied development within a love relationship. It often symbolizes the full bloom of a partnership or a desire for marriage and family. It is a time of harvest.

Family: Related to family matters, the Sun stands for being blessed with children, happiness through children, or an intense longing for them—a fulfilled family life. There is a blessing on the family to be used to advantage. This is a good time for reconciliation, rectification of former wrongs, forgiveness, the return of the "prodigal son." Celebrate with your loved ones! Celebrate without any particular reason, just for yourselves!

Partners/Friends: Projects that you start (again) will succeed. Fruitful impulses coming from outside will benefit all parties concerned. Communication is intensive and creative. Take the time for a vacation together in the sun, relaxing after periods of stress and chaos.

Not conscious: The negative sides indicated by the Sun are finding pleasure in superficial and temporarily pleasant circumstances, excessive living, enjoying a life of luxury by exploiting other people, power trips and greed as an expression of lacking social responsibility, misuse of money and influence.

Key words: Joy in life and earthly fulfillment within partnership, experienced as supernatural grace.

20 The Call

20 The Call

Description and comparison: In the Tarot of Love, two larger-than-life soul birds rule the picture. They attentively observe a couple, protecting them as they stretch their arms up to the heavens toward a powerful rainbow light which bursts from the Tao symbol of yin and yang.

The Rider-Waite Tarot shows a huge angel, reminiscent of card 14, blowing a trumpet. The angel wakes the dead from their graves and raises them from their coffins. Waite called his card Judgment.

As in an Indian rainbow mandala, a smaller and a larger external person are transparently woven into each other in the Crowley Tarot. The deep-blue symbolic form of a primordial mother encloses both of them. Crowley named this card The Aeon.

General: We near the end of our life's journey through and with archetypal forms of behavior and situations. The Sun represents the perfect earthly life. It is time to turn our eyes from the earth and to focus on the higher realms. We hear or feel an inner or outer calling to find completely new dimensions of life. To do so, a new birth or rebirth is necessary, and it is often connected with a judgment on how we have led our lives. This calling comes from our own soul, our self. We should avoid thinking an external power or supernatural authorities to be the source of this call, as in the Entanglement (Devil). Otherwise we might try to evade making our own decision.

The Call reveals to us the divine spark of an immortal consciousness; it contains the promise of a new, different life, a spiritual awakening, and a fountain of youth, which is why in other tarot decks this card is called, for example, The Aeon, Judgment, and Rebirth.

Jesus of Nazareth, who became Christ, followed his calling and conveyed to his followers the message of a new, eternal life through spiritual rebirth. Christopher Columbus followed the call of his adventure and his royal benefactor to discover a new earthly paradise. Martin Luther King followed the call of his heart and human conscience to teach nonviolently righteousness and brotherhood. Mother Theresa has lived her calling in succoring the poor.

Love: Our souls softly whisper to us. Whatever we know about the psychology of love will not help us on the further path of partnership. We are called on to orient ourselves inwardly and to accept wherever our calling leads us, in the partnership or alone.

Love is ultimately founded on the conviction of one common source and one common destiny for all human beings. You can call it God, Tao, Paradise, Truth, or whatever. The Call reminds us to make that theoretical conviction a practical experience by turning inward for meditation and contemplation, by opening up to mystic revelations.

If you draw this card for a functional relationship, it indicates that both partners should now find a new, spiritual destination for the next stages of their soul travel together.

If you draw this card concerning a broken or neglected or co-dependent relationship, it points out the chance to revitalize or reunite if a conscious effort is made—keeping in mind that all differences veil one common basis: the divine essence of all life.

Family: The Call indicates a second or third springtime for the older generation, a new vision for the young. It stands for a call to recognize and appreciate that we can take up more than one role such as mother, father, child, sister, brother, grandparents. We are multi-dimensional beings. We must join forces to attain a common higher goal or ideal. Knowing that we will always remain connected on a spiritual level, we should develop more understanding if a family member follows their very special calling and takes up their own course.

Partners/Friends: Mutual support of partner and friends is the way in which we can attain the desires awakened by the Moon card. The Call helps us to experience, or to extend help during, the process of rebirth, which makes it necessary to give up the ego (some or all of it) and at the same time give our friend reassuring, deep compassion. While 13 Transformation and 16 Lightning embody inevitable events that we have to endure, even if we have caused them ourselves, we do not have to take up the Call. But its promises are magnificent enough for us to look upward and let go of all trivial and irrelevant matters.

Not conscious: We are incapable of coping with the judgment passed by our own conscience or by someone from our environment when we hear the Call for an uplifting attitude toward life or for changes in patterns of behavior. We miss a last chance for transforming ourselves, developing, and opening up to a completely new dimension of consciousness.

Key words: Spiritual rebirth of relationship. A call for a new direction in life. Reorientation. Evaluation of one's path in life.

21 The World

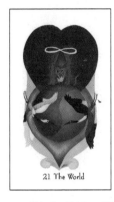

21 The World

Description and comparison: In the Tarot of Love, Gaia or our globe is created from the complete Tao of a blue and green yin and yang joined together, completely encircled by a rainbow aura. Our couple stand serenely on top of this globe under a white lemniscate, the symbol of eternity. They hold each other; flowers blossom between them. The two cranes fly toward each other; the red heart of love reigns supreme.

In the Rider-Waite Tarot, a young woman scantily veiled in a flowing garment dances in a garland with two wands, free in the blue of the endless sky. The four corners of the card reveal the symbols of the four Evangelists: angel (Matthew), eagle (John), bull (Luke), and lion (Mark).

The Crowley Tarot shows a nude, sensually arousing woman dancing lithely in the blue-green source of creation. She supports her foot on the head of a snake which she has conquered or tamed. With a heavenly circle in her hand she "measures" the light flowing from a divine eye. The four corners of the card again show the symbols of the four Evangelists.

General: The search is at an end; we have arrived in our eternal home. The circle of the path and the course of one's life have drawn to a close. The ideal picture of unity and freedom determines the vital consciousness. The game or the dance in the universe is light and carefree. "Problems" are taken on as opportunities for development.

The phoenix of card 13 Transformation has risen for good. It now draws its course in front of the background of an eternal firmament of eternity and immortality. You experience yourself to be a part of the entire creation and of the creator, feeling supported by the cosmic energies.

Adam and Eve are archetypes of this tarot card, as well as the Indian Kali, mother of the gods.

There is not much to say about The World; it is a "simple" card. In contrast to some other interpreters of the tarot, we see 21 The World as being without any gloomy secondary meanings such as complacency, self-righteousness, or stagnation. When the World is seen and experienced as a totality and unity, the *unio mystica,* the mystical union of the soul with God is the focus of the immediate experience.

Love: The card primarily shows that we are on top, no matter what the outer circumstances of our present life might be. The World shows love as a personal and transpersonal relationship. Female and male interests and energies, erotic and spiritual longings can be balanced in a harmonious way.

If an intimate love relationship is not really what you or your partner desire, though you are erotically involved, this would be a good time to transform the relationship into a nonsexual friendship. In contrast to the vigor of the Sun, the World shows a harmoniously balanced love relationship in which feminine and masculine interests, as well as erotic and spiritual wishes are in equilibrium, without having to find expression in an earthy, material form.

The World can symbolize a partnership built on kindness and growing wisdom, as well as the association of two "older" souls who have already lived through too much suffering to want—subconsciously or consciously—to repeat it.

Family: The World stands for the ceaseless continuity of life through the succession of generations. We sense the connection that our parents, grandparents, and ancestors have to our own soul and personality and how we will maintain such a connection with our children and grandchildren. The World can also indicate the birth of a child entering our universe; moving out of the home into a place of one's own or to a foreign country; the independent continuous development of one's life on the secure foundation of a cultural and social unity.

Partners/Friends: Both have found their centers and can now become more actively productive without thinking of money or fame. A new cycle starts in which we can use both inner and outer independence and that which we have learned within the world and for the world. Friends are invisibly protected. They feel their partnership to be an expression of the eternal cycle and of the close bond between their souls.

Not conscious: We sense a positive energy, but do not yet know what to do with it. We do not find the right moment or the courage—or both—to jump off the treadmill of everyday concerns and on to the wheel of life which wants to carry us upward to an unknown destination.

Key words: Completion or perfection of karmic relationship through creative enjoyment of the potential. Harmonious dissolution of relationship.

0 The Fools

0 The Fools

Description and comparison: A man and a woman balance securely on a tightrope spanning the valley of the hearts in the Tarot of Love. They wave happily at each other—is the apparent farewell only temporary? Blossoms and cranes, symbols of emotion and soul, are obviously striving for individual courses of development as well. The position of the sun is held by the Tao sign, symbolizing inner unity.

As usual in most tarot decks, the Rider-Waite Tarot shows an upward-looking young man walking nimbly into what seems to be his ruin: his fall from the world of the safe earth. A small dog follows him. His bundle is small; he does not carry much around with him (as of yet or anymore). The white flower in his hand symbolizes the purity of his heart.

In the Crowley Tarot, garlands of light, a butterfly, a dove, grapes, a crocodile, and a small lion entwine the hermaphroditic figure dressed in green. It has an enraptured look on its face.

General: The number 0 already indicates that the Fools are people who do not fit into the usual scheme of things. There is—according to the level of consciousness—nothing to desire, wish for, and do as of yet, since the Fools are like children. Or there is no longer anything to desire, wish for, or do. Then our Fools are sages.

The Fools stand for independence and the ability to live freely and happily, even when alone. They can mean an uncommitted and irresponsible attitude, again according to the level of consciousness and life experience.

Most tarot decks have only one figure here, a masculine being. In the Tarot of Love we have two people, who embody the positive "enlightened" consciousness of the Fools.

Fools look behind the scenes and expose the weaknesses of tradition, dogmas, and morals. They let the spectators suspect that we are all fools if we continue to remain stuck in social conventions or forms of behavior conditioned by fear— in doing so we are fooling ourselves as to the true nature of human life.

We do not know if Lao Tse was a "fool" in this sense, since no information has been handed down as to whether or not he lived his enlightenment within a partnership or love relationship. Woody Allen and Diane Keaton, as well as Karl Valentin and Liesl Karlstadt have done well as "foolish couples," in films, at least.

Love: The Fools show a perfect freedom of choice as to whether or not, and how, to stay in the relationship, without the inhibitive influences of psychological games, ego trips, or dramatic emotional attachments.

If only one partner lives out this freedom, the relationship will not be easy or even endure for long period of time. The Fool in this partnership will continue to poke "innocently" into old ego wounds.

This card also illustrates the personal greatness and grace to remain unperturbed and even happy during separation from a partner without being bitter and projecting guilt. It is known by one or both of the partners that only living in the here and now really matters. If we go with the flow of life, even problems that seem to be overwhelming can easily be solved, because we are ready to detach ourselves from the problems and do not hold onto them.

The Fools card also indicates the ability to recognize the meaning and purpose of life even when each walks a different path. It means being able to live alone (all-one) for some time.

Family: In terms of the family, the Fools means bidding farewell to rigid structures whose passing need not be mourned. It indicates taking chances in order to develop oneself. You take responsibility for your life, even without the support of family and tradition. Fools experiment with different furniture, new colors and pictures, unusual hobbies, or travel to unknown destinations.

Partners/Friends: Fools are prepared to allow true freedom for themselves and others. They trust in the natural course of life, they can let go. Fools consciously make life easier for themselves and others; they avoid complicating friendships with psychological games or dramas (which are really expressions of a communication gap or a lack of courage to acknowledge emotional desires and the possibility that the partner will not fill them).

Not conscious: In terms of yourself, there is the danger of confusing irresponsibility with freedom, recklessness with adventure, and stupidity with courage and individuality. In terms of others, there is a tendency to (mis-)judge them because they are different and believe in different values. An inability to perceive meaning in unusual or strange behavior of others leads to self-righteous condemnation.

Key words: Illusions about ideal love. Irresponsibility. Realization of truly independent, free love released from karmic bondage, according to the motto, "It doesn't always have to be karma to be love or to love!"

22 Soul Mates

22 Soul Mates

The Rider-Waite Tarot and some other tarot decks include a white card, a "carte blanche," a "joker." Such a card stands for an answer that is not to be determined by drawing the tarot cards with their archetypal images. We are offered the opportunity to deal with the question as we please. In many tarot decks, however, there is no "joker," no extra card.

The Tarot of Love highlights synergy and intimate companionship on all soul levels, identifying the secret or open desire of all human beings for partnership. Artist Marcia Perry expresses this ideal through two large soul cranes which form a dome pointing up to the heavens. It shields the loving encounter of two "external" people, who are held by an open lotus blossom.

Soul Mates is the "carte blanche" in the Tarot of Love. If you draw this card, you deal with transpersonal, celestial, and/or supernatural factors influencing your relationship. You are bound to find a soul mate or a twin soul. We make a point of differentiating between twin souls and soul mates. A twin soul is a person with whom you can identify and share almost 100 percent mutual understanding without any erotic relationship. A soul mate is the person to whom we find ourselves attracted even unwillingly or magnetically and vice versa and with whom we have to learn so many more lessons in life. It is more often than not a very passionate exchange on all levels of our being, including the erotic levels.

If you draw this card you will encounter either a soul mate or a twin soul. Destiny provides you with the rare opportunity of being able to decide spontaneously of your own free will. The relationship for which you drew this card will offer a wealth of profound life experiences. Whatever decision you make is born under a lucky star!

3

The Minor Arcana

Rods, Nuggets, Blossoms, Lightnings: The Four Suits in the Tarot of Love

The fifty-six cards of the Minor Arcana fall into four groups or suits, each with four court cards and ten numbered cards. Tarot literature agrees that the four suits were the forerunners of our common playing cards. Traditional tarot decks have suits of swords (spades), wands or staves (clubs), cups (hearts), and coins, disks, or pentacles (diamonds). The Tarot of Love changes the suits to reflect its own character.

Rods (wands or staves in other decks) are undisputed. They are like staves you can use to lean on, to poke around with in the brushwood or leaves, to defend yourself if necessary, or to show someone something—but they are also magic wands!

Nuggets (disks, pentacles, or coins) have to do with the material structure we extract from the earth element. Nuggets are the glittering gold in its primary form as found in Mother Earth. Gold has always been related to the hope of a life without worries, as well as to robbery, hate, and war. Gold is the absolute symbol of luck, an expression of might and recognition, and it symbolizes the joy of life. Gold is the color of the sun; it reflects the radiance, power, and warmth of the sun. The kind of luck brought by golden insignia of office, rings, bracelets, necklaces, and coins depends primarily on whether or not we are attached to the earthly form, the physical shape in which luck can appear. But that the tangible and visible luster can also make you happy is "legitimate," is a part of human life. This is misunderstood by some New Age devotees who are oriented only toward the other world and too flatly reject material pursuits. The alchemists utilize the process of transforming base metals into rare gold for a good reason.

Blossoms (cups) are soft things that grow within nature, fitting to the element of water. Some authors relate the four suits to Grail mythology, in which a chalice, or cup, symbolizes the mythical Grail. However, we do not want to present an esoteric-occult interpretation in the Tarot of Love. We feel it more important to present a practical approach: how we can more consciously and happily deal with feelings, thoughts, goals, and energies within partnerships. Blossoms often do have a chalice shape, yet they are not fixed in their form. Their flower petals remain soft and flexible. They offer themselves as a colorful revelation of an eternal creative power combining cheerful diversity with unsuspected fertility.

Lightnings (swords) symbolize the sudden, fiery, beneficial or destructive effect of the fire element. Lightnings express flashing, sudden qualities. Swords are an age-old symbol of power and struggle, and, infrequently, of the ability to protect oneself. A sword always cuts. In contrast, lightning is an electrical discharge of overwhelming and concentrated voltage. Lightning has a destructive element, but it can also be the sudden illuminating flash in the darkest night; we humans can probably thank it for the first fire we used. In the Tarot of Love, lightnings symbolize the sudden discharge of tension—known to go along with a violent display of power—which contributes decisively to the clarification of a situation.

New times require new pictures and new symbols. New energies, expanded consciousness, and changes in behavior need new formulas so that we can express and recognize ourselves. Every living thing flows, moves. All people develop, so we continuously need new approaches in order to open heart, mind, and soul for the appropriate impulses and the right creative opportunities.

There is a tendency in esoterics to want to relate everything: tarot with astrology, astrology with numerology, numerology with the kabbalah, the kabbalah with tarot, and so on. This sometimes works very well, but too often it is a strain to look for forced cross-connections, only to come up with a closed system. It is true that everything is connected. But how? Perhaps not necessarily according to the rules of analytical, one-dimensional logic or to the spontaneous perceptions of supposed cosmic messages and intuitions. Possibly there are no direct references that can be seen and understood in a linear way or that might be immediately envisioned. Why should we not accept that large parts of our human lives remain a mystery? "Life is not a problem that we must solve, but rather a secret which we can experience," as one saying goes. Another saying is, "Life is not a problem to be solved, but a mystery to be lived."

Since the four elements of fire, air, water, and earth are powerful forces in life, it helps to link them with the suits of the tarot. As the correspondences of the four tarot suits with the four elements vary in tarot literature, no interpretation should be taken as more than a guide.

In the Tarot of Love, blossoms correspond to the water element, its versatility, softness, and living fertility.

We prospect for gold in the earth; the earth reflects the golden rays of the sun. Nuggets (coins, which represent the value of metal won from the earth) are the concentrated image of the earth element.

Rods, according to some writers, stand for fire (with swords corresponding to air). We do not think that this is comprehensible. For example, why should the leafy wooden rods (wands) of the Rider-Waite Tarot be fiery? Fire is power, might, the ambivalent effect of violence—for the benefit or detriment of humanity. This exactly suits the character of lightnings (swords). Rods can be used to hit, but they are primarily seen and used as supports, pointers, or magic wands. Air is exchange, osmosis, the medium of which all people partake; we will someday breath in what other people have breathed out.

Key Words for the Four Suits

Rods: Exchange, air, energy, and ideals. Idealistic motivation. Opportunity to change through one's own inner impulses. Spiritual-ethereal love. Pulsating, intuitive energy. Not conscious: Lost creative opportunities.

Nuggets: Property, earth, energy, and structure. Material motivation. External enrichment. Sensual-earthy love. Fixed, physical energy. Not conscious: Materialistic lifestyle.

Blossoms: Accommodation, water, energy, and sensation. Emotional motivation. Inner enrichment. Erotic-emotional love. Flowing, psychic energy. Not conscious: Losing oneself in emotions.

Lightnings: Power, fire, energy, and thoughts. Mental motivation. Necessity of change through external conflict. Sexual-aggressive love. Polarizing, magnetic energy. Not conscious: Mentally fixated lifestyle.

We differentiate between the idealistic motivation and intuitive-pulsating energy of rods-air, and the mental motivation and polarizing, magnetic energy of lightnings-fire.

The Court or Personality Cards:
Reflections of Dominant Characteristics
and Capabilities

The terms king, queen, prince, and princess are also not universal. Most tarot decks have knights, which correspond to our prince. The Crowley Tarot deck's prince corresponds to the king of the Tarot of Love. The pages of traditional tarot decks are called princesses in the Tarot of Love.

Queens and kings, princes and princesses represent personified aspects of certain traits, abilities, and ego strategies. Unlike the figures of the Major Arcana, which often act as inevitable fate, the figures of the court cards are controllable. The court cards stand between the archetypal figures of the Major Arcana and the numbered cards of the Minor Arcana, to which they formally belong. You will find only human figures in the personality cards, which represent condensations of elements or temperaments.

The court cards are clearly recognized images of firmly defined qualities and attitudes toward life. They symbolically relate to the orientation toward which the person asking the question would like to or should strive or which they have already actualized and now live out.

When we draw one or more court cards, they refer to us personally or to people who play a role in our lives. They can also deal with aspects of the personality or persons who will become important to us in the near future. When a personality card appears, people, topics, and problems can be clearly identified, even personalized.

Key Words for the Court Cards

Queen: The opportunity for mastery of the feminine powers. The yin aspect of a relationship. The mother. The anima.

King: The opportunity for mastery of the masculine powers. The yang aspect of a relationship. The father. The animus.

Prince: The effort to rule, promote, and herald (communicate) the yang powers. The awakening animus.

Princess: The effort to rule, promote, and herald (communicate) the yin powers. The awakening anima.

SUIT OF RODS

Queen of Rods

Queen of Rods

General: The woman questioner should or can more strongly accept her femininity and take the inner throne that she deserves. The man questioner has the opportunity—or is challenged—to keep consciously in contact with his feminine energy, the anima.

Example: Shirley MacLaine, who has the courage to live her own truth—and publish it!

Love: Intuitive, animated ability to love based on spiritual harmony. A decisive woman enters our life.

Family: The elemental powers of the primordial mother find worldly expression in a dominant woman with leadership abilities.

Partners/Friends: The inwardly independent woman is an equal, a complementary partner and friend.

Not conscious: Suppression of one's own femininity. The challenge of being intuitively led by the feminine principle.

King of Rods

King of Rods

General: Inspirations through ideas and creative projections, as well as the task of making them concrete. The woman asking the question should externalize even more powerfully abilities already acquired.

Examples: Herbert von Karajan, the conductor, a sovereign of musical presentation with the baton as his magic wand. Ted Turner who against all odds built a global information network based on human values.

Love: Masculine, yang power can direct love toward a goal that inspires both partners. We meet a man who is important to us.

Family: The patriarch who derives his authority from intellectual superiority. The understanding father.

Partners/Friends: Assistance from a mature man. Matured concepts and plans.

Not conscious: Good ideas and plans are not realized; powers dissolve in thin air. Help is not recognized when one has problems with masculine authority.

Prince of Rods

Prince of Rods

General: Youthful elan applied to ideas with youthful elan. Ability to intelligently, quickly communicate.

Example: John F. Kennedy, who inspired a whole generation with his youthful personality and his fresh presentation of common ideals.

Love: When a woman is asking the question, the prince stands for the desire for more independence or the wish for a man who can give love new wings. When a man is asking the question: the desire or ability to scintillate with youthful charm.

Family: Even suggestions that are not yet ripe should be given attention. Possibly male offspring, an awaited prince.

Partners/Friends: Brainstorming, a good time for creative exchange.

Not conscious: Striving for more notice from the external world. Possibly, conflicts about opposing opinions and ideologies.

Princess of Rods

Princess of Rods

General: The carefree restlessness of a teenager who wants to discover and experience his or her identity.

Example: Steffi Graf, a champion in women's tennis. She follows her goals with drive and concentration, and is graceful in doing so. The tennis racquet is her magic wand.

Love: Shyly falling in love for the first time, not on one's own initiative. Possibly, platonic love. A young woman may enter our life.

Family: Someone needs silent spiritual support, even if what s/he wants is not clear to her/him.

Partners/Friends: All thoughts and plans that promise more joy in life are beneficial.

Not conscious: We turn in circles and are caught up in our own unreal expectations, which often remain unreal even to ourselves.

SUIT OF NUGGETS

Queen of Nuggets

Queen of Nuggets

General: The art of handling property and structures profitably, sensibly, and humanely. Inner and outer riches.

Examples: Queen Elizabeth II of England, if we think only of wealth and position. The mythological Gaia, Earth Mother and primordial mother, the richly giving ruler of this planet, is the ancestress of all the queens of nuggets.

Love: Resolutely powerful, sensual ability to love. A natural attitude toward sexuality without false shame.

Family: Cautious, protective family-mindedness. Cozy home.

Partners/Friends: Warm-hearted care for the well-being of others.

Not conscious: Oppressive mothering instinct. Appreciating only materialistic aspects.

King of Nuggets

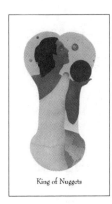

King of Nuggets

General: Security based on tradition and possessions. Reliability. Generosity. Talent for ruling over property.

Examples: The Sultan of Brunei, ruler of a small oil country in the Pacific basin, is said to be the richest man in the world. Also Emperor Charles V, in whose domain the sun never set because his empire stretched from Europe to South America.

Love: Sovereign joys and gifts of love. A hedonist.

Family: A patriarch who pays attention to the well-being of his loved ones. Social recognition.

Partners/Friends: Good prerequisite for financially secure plans. Realistic approach to life.

Not conscious: Striving to dominate other people's material factors. Miserliness. Spiritual rigidity through lifestyle that is only earthbound and physical.

Prince of Nuggets

Prince of Nuggets

General: Unbridled ambition to attain a sense of self-worth and individual identity. Exercising power through visible possessions.

Example: Donald Trump, the real-estate tycoon of New York.

Love: There is a decision to be made as to whether you give more priority to inner or external values. For a woman, possible prospect of a so-called "good catch."

Family: Active help from a youth in contributing to livelihood.

Partners/Friends: Opportunity for great, mutual financial success.

Not conscious: Spiritual bankruptcy. Pushy mentality. Risky business deals. Living beyond our means.

Princess of Nuggets

Princess of Nuggets

General: The promise of earthly happiness in every respect. Someone who attracts attention in the gray of everyday life.

Example: Gloria von Thurn und Taxis, of jet-set fame, continuously provides the press with new escapades and extravagances, like a bird of paradise among blackbirds.

Love: Sensuality couples with joy of life. Youth with a healthy striving for prosperity. Longing for adventure.

Family: New joy of motherhood. Striving for comfort.

Partners/Friends: Fortuna laughs very unexpectedly.

Not conscious: Tendency toward wastefulness. Possible infidelity or boredom in the partnership. Disappointment in partner's lack of quality.

SUIT OF BLOSSOMS

Queen of Blossoms

Queen of Blossoms

General: Living by way of feelings, from the heart.

Examples: Sophia Loren and Brigitte Bardot have formed an entire film epoch and the image of woman for both sexes. They are passionate, warm-hearted, sensitive, and self-confident. The romance novelist Barbara Cartland also belongs to the queens of blossoms.

Love: When a man draws this card, he either needs or longs for a full-blooded woman. If a woman draws it, she can (or should) live out her femininity in an erotic-emotional manner.

Family: An emotional person who can open-heartedly give and take. A loving atmosphere.

Partners/Friends: Help through intuitive faculties, perhaps through a woman who is a psychic.

Not conscious: Identity dissolves because too much is uncritically absorbed and adopted. An excessive mother-hen mentality.

King of Blossoms

King of Blossoms

General: Ambitious representation of feelings; sensitive treatment of other people.

Examples: Julio Iglesias and Valentino Liberace. A king of blossoms rules over the hearts of women without breaking them! Women worshipped these two men even when they had reached an advanced age.

Love: For a woman, the fulfillment of secret love desires. For a man, perhaps the nicest qualities a man can have.

Family: The loving, kind father does not need to make a secret of his soft side.

Partners/Friends: Musical, artistic tendencies and abilities. A patron.

Not conscious: A person "without a backbone." A cold, hard-hearted withdrawal from feelings.

Prince of Blossoms

Prince of Blossoms

General: Premonition and promise of blossoming love.

Examples: The medieval troubadours and the legendary Casanova, heralds of love who not only sang about or awoke yearning but also knew how to satisfy it. Casanova was not the irresponsible heart-breaker that a peevish, bourgeois morality would like to brand him, but was rather a sincere lover of the world who was documented to look after the well-being of his lovers even when the affairs were over.

Love: When a woman draws this card, it indicates a younger man, perhaps a romantic liaison. A man who draws this card can or should give more space to his romantic affairs.

Family: Unusual talent which is still looking for its proper expression in a (male?) member of the family.

Partners/Friends: The ability to accept and adapt to the feelings of others.

Not conscious: Misused charm. Purposely leaving other people in the dark as to feelings, or playing with feelings. Fear of making a commitment, or unwillingness or inability to make a commitment.

Princess of Blossoms

Princess of Blossoms

General: Tender sentiments, poetic awareness of life.

Examples: Snow White, Sleeping Beauty, and the princess who slept on the pea. Highly sensitive, they live in a fairy-tale world of feelings and wait for the liberating kiss of the prince.

Love: First erotic happiness in love, first fulfillment. Need for tenderness. The wish to revive previous happiness.

Family: Long-cherished dreams or wishes can come true, sustained by harmonious vibrations. Mutual feelings of happiness. Possibly female offspring.

Partners/Friends: Vivacious energies of young femininity bubble like champagne and animate the partner with new creativity.

Not conscious: Attempt to hold onto something that is gone. Presenting oneself as more weak and passive than one really is in order to manipulate other people. Over-sensitivity.

SUIT OF LIGHTNINGS

Queen of Lightnings

Queen of Lightnings

General: Fiercely demanding female intelligence. Sudden occurrences having to do with women.

Example: Indira Gandhi, the prime minister of India who seemed to dominate her country like the Hindu goddess Durga riding on the tiger; however, unlike the goddess, Gandhi fell victim to her position of power.

Love: Aggressive love that does not avoid a polarization. Men still often flinch around such women; women are often startled when they discover this energy in themselves. Finding pleasure in open sexuality. Encountering a racy, self-confident woman.

Family: The woman claims her (legitimate) rights; she forces mental conflicts and changes to come about.

Partners/Friends: Overwhelming ability to attract others and to assert oneself through courage or magnetic powers.

Not conscious: Fury. Self-righteous conflicts. Emotional coldness. Craftiness.

King of Lightnings

King of Lightnings

General: Furious power in the development of mental sketches and systems. Sudden occurrences related to a man.

Example: Wilhelm Reich, the revolutionary researcher and psychologist. He was on the track of the source of all vital energies, from sexuality to *prana* or "Od." He experimented with radioactivity and rain-making. Right up until his death he was persecuted, sued, and branded as an intellectual subversive because his achievements seemed to threaten established views of the world.

Love: Vehement sex urge and pleasure in experimentation, possibly also a longing for these.

Family: Influences follow the motto "hard but just." Great devotion to the well-being of the family.

Partners/Friends: Joint thoughts can be energetically put into action.

Not conscious: Hurtful behavior, possibly without awareness of its effects. Unkindness.

Prince of Lightnings

Prince of Lightnings

General: The mood for change. Excessive energies search for the right outlet. Unusual stamina when standing up for something, in spreading a conviction.

Example: Michael Jackson, who captured the trend of a certain spirit of the time with his provocative lyrics and well-orchestrated performances in music videos and on stage.

Love: Carefree drive for love which seeks to be lived out. An unusually attractive man.

Family: Excitement, challenge through willful actions.

Partners/Friends: Stimulating impulses from unexpected sources.

Not conscious: Power is wasted. Superficial action. Anarchistic defiance.

Princess of Lightnings

Princess of Lightnings

General: One is easily motivated to action by rational thoughts. Surprising turns in thinking, speaking, and action.

Example: Jane Fonda. The spectrum of her interests and abilities extends from the much-courted *Barbarella* film star full of sparkling eroticism to the committed anti-war propagandist to the Academy award-winning actress in *Klute* to the successful representative of a fitness trend—all of which she continues to transform even further.

Love: Fascination through sexual fantasies. First experience of feminine fiery love or the desiring of it. Amazons and Valkyries, the fighting virgins of Greek and Germanic antiquity, belong to this card, as do spirited, youthful women in general.

Family: Animating influence through unvarnished naturalness of expression. New joy in life through witty, sudden actions.

Partners/Friends: Unexpected inspirations. Ability to be enthusiastic.

Not conscious: Unreflected contradiction. Flightiness.

The Numbered Cards:
Reflections of Passing States of Mind and External Influences

A critical look at interpretations accompanying popular tarot decks and in books shows that, for example, cards numbered five are almost always said to be negative, regardless of their suit. The Crowley Tarot deck titles five of cups Disappointment, five of swords Defeat, five of disks Worry and five of wands Strife. The cards numbered ten are also frequently given negative interpretations, with the notion that "all energy ends here" (Crowley Tarot). But energy naturally never ends and the ten is one on a higher decade. There are no cards which are negative, just as there are no negative numbers. Why should five be "worse" than other numbers? Why should the five members of a hand, the five elements (earth, water, fire, air, and ether—the element of human beings), the five senses, the five planets which we can see with the naked eye (Mercury, Venus, Mars, Jupiter, Saturn) be related to worries, troubles, evil premonitions, and the like?

Indeed, the images on the cards are completely subjective, ultimately arbitrary illustrations of very personal emotions—in traditional decks as well as in the Tarot of Love. The cards possess no authority or competence higher than any other way of looking at things.

This is why we do not base the Tarot of Love on the traditional interpretations that are hard to understand or are gloomy, negative ways of looking at the world and fearful attitudes toward life. We offer an approach to the tarot that is consistent, open, and comprehensible to everyone, and can be harmonized with the person asking the question and their concerns, thereby imparting a positive, constructive view of life.

As we should not eat food which does not taste good or

which harms us, we should not take on from outside of ourselves feelings or thoughts that do not have a positive basis.

Key Words for the Numbered Cards

Ace: New beginning. Awakening. Primary energy.

Two: Encounter. Yin-yang. Polarity.

Three: Productive organization. Constructive creativity.

Four: Forming. Securing. Strength.

Five: Mediation. Communication. Decision. New orientation.

Six: Harmony. Joy in life. Sensitivity.

Seven: Radical change. Necessity for new orientation and for change.

Eight: Wealth. Abundance. Living flow of energy.

Nine: Conclusion. Completion. Detachment. Meditation.

Ten: Opening up. Continuing on higher level. Self-determination.

Perhaps you will find further key words for the numbers. Use them in the manner which intuitively feels right to you.

SUIT OF RODS

Ace of Rods

Ace of Rods

General: Manifestation of new ideas and ideals. Opportunity for deep spiritual harmony.

Love: Intuitive harmony of vibrations. Soul mates, spiritual love. United by an idea. Creative love.

Family: A new mutual spiritual focus.

Partners/Friends: Appreciating the same ideals.

Not conscious: Communication comes to a halt.

Two of Rods

Two of Rods

General: Collecting experience through spiritual encounters. Opportunity to develop consciously masculine and feminine qualities in yourself through association with others.

Love: Opportunity to recognize the interplay of yin and yang in encountering the opposite sex.

Family: Impulse to communicate with family members individually and directly.

114

Partners/Friends: Opportunity to fulfill the goals which you strive for together.

Not conscious: Danger of blocking yourself in the partnership by projecting your own negative vibrations on the other person and then clinging to the resulting distorted picture and reflection.

Three of Rods

Three of Rods

General: Development of creative ideas and ideals. Concrete formulation of creative plans.

Love: Making mutual plans. Possible desire for children.

Family: Ability and willingness to work constructively together.

Partners/Friends: Striving for a common goal.

Not conscious: Not recognizing or missing the opportunity of giving expression to creative impulses.

Four of Rods

General: Putting ideas into action, carrying out plans.

Love: Powerful coming together of mutual intentions.

Family: Keeping the small group together through formulation of common values and goals in living together.

Partners/Friends: Clearly determined cooperation in working toward the goals of the relationship.

Not conscious: The strong wish for finding form and security is neurotically exaggerated and can lead to narrowing and fixation of consciousness, to mental straitjackets and rigid ideas.

Five of Rods

General: Openness to and communication about new ideas and ideals.

Love: Intellectual exchange about the relationship, new point of view, and re-evaluation of what you have in common.

Family: New perspectives for living together.

Partners/Friends: Opportunity to change plans.

Not conscious: Confusion in the relationship because of being flooded by too many different mental impulses. Inability to make decisions. "Swimming with the tide."

Six of Rods

Six of Rods

General: Harmonic spiritual vibration, joy of life founded on spirituality.

Love: Flexible stability in the relationship. Inspiration. Sensitivity. Private happiness.

Family: Interplay of ideals.

Partners/Friends: Ideas and plans bear fruit.

Not conscious: Closed to harmonic vibrations and energies, which can be used. "Missing the boat" to happiness.

Seven of Rods

Seven of Rods

General: Doubting values or course in life. Necessity of examining your own point of view and expanding it. Possibly going separate ways (for a time).

Love: Apparently because of external influences, the spiritual foundation and the self-expression of each person must be redefined or deepened. Opportunity or pressure for starting anew.

Family: The need to recognize the individuality of every family member and to allow them private space.

Partners/Friends: Stability and center must be found in yourself, not in others.

Not conscious: There are crises: through separation (or the intention to do so), through the seemingly unpredictable imperilment of a mutual ideal, or through other upsets to the relationship.

Eight of Rods

Eight of Rods

General: Opening up to cosmic visions of ideal life, which can also result in earthly riches.

Love: Lively joy in spiritual love. High spirits, exuberant happiness.

Family: The blessings of domestic happiness.

Partners/Friends: Harmony, the vibrations of which can assist other people.

Not conscious: Unquenched longing for spiritual fulfillment.

Nine of Rods

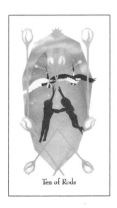

Nine of Rods

General: Recognition of greater correlations. Spiritual contemplation and transformation.

Love: Opportunity of recognizing old, restrictive patterns of behavior and discarding them. Learning to appreciate inner values. Achieving mutual goals.

Family: Dissolving and freeing oneself from outdated structures and role-playing.

Partners/Friends: Consistent completion of plans. Leaving rigid forms of relationships.

Not conscious: Dissolutions and endings seem to be forced on you externally, by "circumstances." Quarreling with your own fate.

Ten of Rods

Ten of Rods

General: Breakthrough to higher dimensions of consciousness allows new ideals to be perceived.

Love: Possibility of mutually putting ideas and ideals into action. Intuitive communication between partners.

Family: New view of the fateful (karmic) relationships within the family. Ability and willingness to give the family a new meaning.

Partners/Friends: New challenges and new goals.

Not conscious: Missing opportunities for achieving new aspects of the partnership on a higher plane.

SUIT OF NUGGETS

Ace of Nuggets

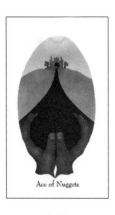

Ace of Nuggets

General: Manifesting material energies. Solid material foundation for mutual projects.

Love: Agreement of physical, worldly interests. Stimulus for sensuous love. Partners are reconnected through a common activity.

Family: A new worldly goal for all, for example, a new house or a vacation with the whole family.

Partners/Friends: An opportunity to work out and realize a profitable plan.

Not conscious: Failure to recognize and utilize first-time or unique opportunities to create a new material foundation.

Two of Nuggets

Two of Nuggets

General: Two material desires face each other. A challenge to decide on principles having to do with physical matters.

Love: Necessity to acknowledge physical desires of both the female and the male partners and to justify them, in terms, for example, of work, having a nice home. Earthy love.

Family: Challenge to clarify together issues of money, property, and possessions.

Partner/Friends: Differing opinions on material values prompt clearing and releasing processes.

Not conscious: Conflict, possibly separation, because of material possessions, money, and so on.

Three of Nuggets

Three of Nuggets

General: Creative handling of physical energies. Plans can be put into reality.

Love: Building a new foundation for one's life. Focused assignment of creative energies.

Family: Pregnancy, birth. New approach to living together.

Partners/Friends: Promising outlook for a mutual project.

Not conscious: Lack of readiness to follow up on good opportunities to improve creatively our worldly living conditions.

Four of Nuggets

Four of Nuggets

General: Stabilizing and safe-guarding material income and property status. Efforts to acquire or enhance comfortable living.

Love: Sound and "safe" relationship.

Family: Affirmed structures, functions, and roles.

Partners/Friends: Strong bonding. Financial success.

Not conscious: Fixation on material values. Avarice. The relationship becomes stagnant and rigid because it is being dominated by material concerns.

Five of Nuggets

Five of Nuggets

General: Chance to gain a new approach toward physical energies and material security. Multitude of new opportunities.

Love: Be ready for changing the material basis of your relationship.

Family: Each person may seek an individual way to external security and enrichment.

Partners/Friends: Impulses to look for a new level of cooperation. New offers.

Not conscious: Worry about securing a living. Fear of poverty. Indecisiveness.

Six of Nuggets

Six of Nuggets

General: Success in worldly affairs. Harmonious management of material energies.

Love: Sensuous, romantic love. Outer success and inner fulfillment can be balanced.

Family: Serene detachment on the basis of a sound financial situation. Plain good luck.

Partners/Friends: In a relaxed atmosphere you can achieve material gains.

Not conscious: Risk of becoming complacent in success or harmony.

Seven of Nuggets

Seven of Nuggets

General: Doubting the continuation and the meaning of physical existence and material values.

Love: Both partners feel obligated to explore and live out their own desires.

Family: Seemingly through outer circumstances, family members are pushed forward to seek out new, individual ways to secure their material existence.

Partners/Friends: Doubting the resilience of common goals. Questioning past successes.

Not conscious: Fear of failure. The earthly foundations of the relationship seem to be seriously endangered. If we do not face the challenge of securing or adapting to the material basis of our life, we may be confronted with major upheavals later on. Possibly, separation because of worldly issues.

Eight of Nuggets

Eight of Nuggets

General: Balanced physical energies are at our disposal. Orderly bounty.

Love: The relationship will "work" erotically. A stroke of luck may bring you wealth. Mutual success. Luxury.

Family: Happiness within the family because of well-structured living conditions.

Partners/Friends: Continuous business expansion is within reach. Happy sharing in the partner's success.

Not conscious: Abuse or squandering of earthly resources.

Nine of Nuggets

Nine of Nuggets

General: Completion of worldly issues. Release from an outlook that is dominated by materialism.

Love: Achieving common earthly goals. Assessment of physical and financial dependencies.

Family: Growing independence from worldly considerations.

Partners/Friends: A chance for mutual support in detaching from materialistic patterns of behavior.

Not conscious: Being blocked by or insisting on remaining in memories of past accomplishment or status. Regret that past good fortune did not persist.

Ten of Nuggets

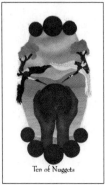

Ten of Nuggets

General: Creation of material living conditions. Shaping new structures "out of nothing."

Love: The relationship will witness a breakthrough toward new goals in life and new opportunities to fulfill material desires.

Family: We see through earthly role-playing and find new common causes.

Partners/Friends: A challenge to shape the partnership and the environment yourselves.

Not conscious: Continuation of outdated materialistic roles. Fateful bonding to unrealized earthly desires.

SUIT OF BLOSSOMS

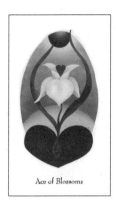

Ace of Blossoms

Ace of Blossoms

General: Rich emotional life. Experiencing new levels and ways of expression. New beginning for emotions.

Love: Desire for erotic love, also the capability for it. Union. Fertility.

Partners/Friends: Intuitive orientation toward harmony in the partnership.

Not conscious: Unclear or unrealistic wishful thinking leads one to believe in a consensus of feelings that is not there.

Two of Blossoms

Two of Blossoms

General: Intense, positive exchange of feelings.

Love: Being in love. Flow of energy. Erotic storm and desire.

Family: Handling each other with kindness.

Partners/Friends: A new encounter leads to fascination.

Not conscious: Being hardened prevents continually experiencing the partner and friends anew. Closing oneself to new emotional dimensions.

Three of Blossoms

Three of Blossoms

General: Unison of feelings can be translated into productive, practical experience.

Love: Pregnancy, birth. Easy, natural harmony in the relationship.

Family: Time of well-being and fulfillment.

Partners/Friends: A third party can be inspired to take part in plans.

Not conscious: Impression of being at a disadvantage in life.

Four of Blossoms

Four of Blossoms

General: Making sure of other people's feelings. Giving clear expression to feelings.

Love: Feelings find form in a partnership (for example, in marriage). Building a life-long partnership on the basis of sensibilities that have a similar direction.

Family: Stable order through harmony on the emotional level.

Partners/Friends: Emotional strength of partnership can be used creatively, artistically, for example.

Not conscious: Attempts to make feelings last forever or to cling to ties lead to disappointment, pain, and possibly separation. Projection of guilt feelings.

Five of Blossoms

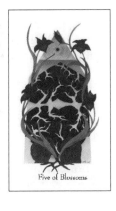

Five of Blossoms

General: Perception of confusing diversity of feelings, emotional reactions, and patterns of behavior.

Love: The feelings you have had up to now are called into doubt by new impulses or external circumstances. Opportunity for a new emotional orientation.

Family: Change in family feelings through new people or energies.

Partners/Friends: Factors unknown up to now can enrich and spur on the partnership.

Not conscious: Disappointment about unexpected fluctuations in the partner's feelings. Confusion in the face of an unclear and complex emotional situation. Not being clear about your own feelings.

Six of Blossoms

Six of Blossoms

General: High spirits. Exuberant feelings. Harmoniously balanced emotional world.

Love: Emotional and erotic joy of life. Satisfaction. Easy exchange of feelings. Ability to be sensitive with partner.

Family: Festive mood. Helping each other on the basis of heartfelt affection.

Partners/Friends: Vivacious time together. Free and easy emotional attachment.

Not conscious: Danger of superficiality in emotional relationship. Deceiving others or self about emotional motivations.

Seven of Blossoms

Seven of Blossoms

General: Disruption of emotional world. Destruction of illusions. Being forced to examine feelings consciously.

Love: Challenge of giving feelings a meaning that is more than personal.

Family: Natural effects of wear and habit in mutual devotion require every family member to reflect on the development of their own emotional patterns and their contribution to the family.

Partners/Friends: Opportunity to concentrate more on yourself and consciously observe the flow of emotional energies.

Not conscious: Cutting off your own energies through excessively living out feelings. Blind hunt for supposed emotional riches. Giving way to almost every emotional impulse.

Eight of Blossoms

Eight of Blossoms

General: Overflowing feelings, as if from an eternal source. Emotional happiness.

Love: Love can be enjoyed like the nectar from a flower.

Family: Feeling secure as a member of an almost endless chain of generations.

Partners/Friends: Prospects for harmonious energy and lively, varied experiences.

Not conscious: Believing that your every emotion is already an expression of cosmic power and inspiration. Danger of becoming too rigid in dogmatically valuing your own sentiments (as do many of the so-called "channels," for example).

Nine of Blossoms

Nine of Blossoms

General: Inner contentment makes emotional ease possible. Fulfillment of hopes and wishes.

Love: Erotic fulfillment of desire for love. Sensing inner emotional bonds not perceived until now. Letting go externally.

Family: Opportunity for deepening of family life. Trying out paths to new freedom. Expanding the emotional world.

Partners/Friends: Natural close of a cycle or process, possibly separation. Grappling with feelings, through meditation or in a psychotherapy group, for example.

Not conscious: Emotional desolation or crippling caused by not discarding or even recognizing old patterns of behavior and feelings. Inability to open up to new emotional impulses. Possibly coldness.

Ten of Blossoms

Ten of Blossoms

General: New sensibility. Spiritualized perceptions. Advance into the dimensions of free emotions.

Love: A love felt to be complete. Freedom from emotional attachments and ego trips.

Family: Mature treatment of other family members, and of your emotions and the emotions of the others.

Partners/Friends: Overcoming hindrances through exchange of emotional energies.

Not conscious: Wanting to pressure others by using your sensibilities. Emotional blocks or outbursts.

SUIT OF LIGHTNINGS

Ace of Lightnings

Ace of Lightnings

General: Influx of new energies. A higher power favors success. Victory. Sense of justice. Sexual love with magnetic attraction.

Love: The relationship is intellectually clarified through conscious grappling with new impulses and/or new powers. A new love may strike like lightning.

Family: Sudden changes in family life.

133

Partners/Friends: Opportunity to carry out plans.

Not conscious: Lack of willingness to deal with strong energies or sudden changes can lead to confusion or collapse.

Two of Lightnings

Two of Lightnings

General: A field of tension is built up. Two powers face each other attentively, without a fight. Taking a position. Balance.

Love: Cautious attitude. Sacrificing realization for at least a period of time. Both poles in the relationship can be clearly recognized.

Family: Willingness to discuss openly controversial issues.

Partners/Friends: Motivations are taken into account. Each partner's strength is (still) peacefully measured against the other's.

Not conscious: Necessary position-taking is avoided. Trying to get out of the clarification process at hand. Convictions are suppressed. Rigid confrontation.

Three of Lightnings

Three of Lightnings

General: Productive handling of ideas and energies which are as quick as lightning.

Love: Flaming passion.

Family: Powerful, fiery cooperation on the basis of inspiring flashes of genius.

Partners/Friends: Necessity of dealing with the energies and ideas of third parties.

Not conscious: Boredom in the relationship. There is nothing (more) to say to each other.

Four of Lightnings

Four of Lightnings

General: Mental powers are brought into a fixed order. Willingness to defend aggressively the basics of life.

Love: Securing one's happiness against external claims, irritations, and dangers.

Family: Being sufficient unto oneself.

Partners/Friends: Trying to insulate mutual ideas against outside influences. Massive power in achieving goals.

Not conscious: Trying to force intellectual order to come about—in resistance to the lightning-quick influx of new energies. Trying (in vain) to close yourself off against sudden external changes.

Five of Lightnings

Five of Lightnings

General: Decisions are to be made. Impulses for risks or adventures. Fighting for the essentials—for the quintessence (*quinta* is Latin for "fifth").

Love: Willingness to adapt with all five senses to changes in the relationship and to have a fiery response.

Family: Desire to overcome rigid structures, if necessary, by using strong powers.

Partners/Friends: New mental orientation. Individual reorientation is due. Mediating disputes.

Not conscious: Fragmentation of concentration and strength. Inaccuracy.

Six of Lightnings

Six of Lightnings

General: Sensitive handling of energies that press for success. Harmonious exchange of powers.

Love: Mutual pleasure in the polarization of conditions of suspense. Enjoyable experience of sexual stimuli. Being certain of the relationship's mesh.

Family: Harmony in the creative balance of individual energies. Holidays from the struggle for existence.

Partners/Friends: Joy in physical activity, such as a common

136

sport. Focusing strength for a success yet to be achieved.

Not conscious: Sweeping existing differences under the rug "for the sake of peace" and trying to even out opposing tendencies.

Seven of Lightnings

Seven of Lightnings

General: Being forced to deal consciously with aggression or a drive for power. Possibly, unstable health.

Love: Fateful upheaval in the relationship: "circumstances" force clarification of aggressive energies. The seven-year itch!

Family: Earlier false behavior must be clarified together or separately.

Partners/Friends: Each must square off with him or her self before the partnership can be fruitful.

Not conscious: Conflict which appears to be insoluble because you feel constantly attacked or you react aggressively.

Eight of Lightnings

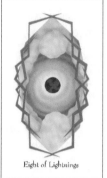

Eight of Lightnings

General: Ability to use lightning-like energy peaks, which occur in the eternal pulse of vibrations, to assert your own interests. Chances for success through quick-wittedness and fast reactions.

Love: Lively flow of energy in the scope of a secure and open relationship. Love which still—or again—"clicks." Harmonious rhythm of giving and taking.

Family: Earlier in-fighting has ended; now is the time to pull together and (again) enjoy living with each other, since differences of opinion have been recognized and can be respected.

Partners/Friends: On the basis of common struggles that have been successfully weathered, you can rest on your laurels or go on to new, exciting plans.

Not conscious: Earlier differences are given too much weight. Lack of willingness to open up to equal powers that are more than personal.

Nine of Lightnings

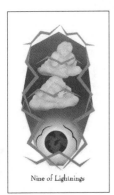

Nine of Lightnings

General: Call to reflect meditatively on aggressions. Serenity. Opportunity to free yourself from a one-sided attitude in a conflict.

Love: Selfless efforts on the part of others at the same time as you consciously forego the assertion of your own interests. Separating without fighting.

Family: Due to family members growing tired of constant fighting or because of improved insight, the weapons are laid down; all can achieve inwardly that which is not possible to achieve externally.

Partners/Friends: The partnership becomes more intimate because an easy mutual understanding grows in addition to intellectual closeness. Parting.

Not conscious: Despair because of constant conflicts. You have no patience with yourself or you torment yourself. Conflicts that seem to have no solution.

Ten of Lightnings

Ten of Lightnings

General: Giving up earthly struggles can lead to an opening of consciousness to higher powers. Worldly challenges are mastered and overcome.

Love: Energies are again united. Active work on mutual karma.

Family: Fresh cosmic-magnetic powers give family life a new direction.

Partners/Friends: Setting off to new shores, in as far as powers of consciousness from a higher dimension can be directed at a mutual goal.

Not conscious: Stagnation in flow of energy. Superiority is wickedly or thoughtlessly used to harm others, which in turn harms oneself.

We have now reached the conclusion of our advice on interpretation. It should naturally be seen only as a primer. You will find your own style and your own way of interpreting the tarot. Your condition of consciousness, your motivations, your present emotional situation, and naturally the questions with which you are concerned will be always be reflected in the cards.

4

Tarot Sessions
and Card-laying Techniques

Tarot as an Energy Process

The origins of most popular spreads are just as impenetrable as the veils that lie over the origins of the tarot. We do not want to add any speculations of our own.

Among the many techniques for laying the cards, none of them is fundamentally superior or inferior. You may, of course, devise your own new spreads. You can also use the spreads given here when you work with other cards, not only with the cards of the Tarot of Love.

Every tarot session—whether with a card reader, in a group, or alone—serves to help us know ourselves. We consider new aspects of our situation; we can clearly picture solutions to our problems and possibilities for development.

Our lives are a complex combination of energy—within ourselves, between partners, within society, in nature, in the entire creation. Conscious people sense life to be a cosmic game of changes. Many of us continue to experience it as a puzzling or frightening drama.

The tarot's world of archetypes is full of dynamic reflections of the conscious and unconscious parts of our lives. These pictures contain the power to release from within new energies that we can use very practically and positively.

We must, however, be prepared to open up to the vibrations of the cards—and to ourselves. We should put ourselves in the right frame of mind for our situation, the question or problem, the tarot cards, the technique of card laying, even the ambience of the session.

Laying the Tarot Cards

Some tarot experts recommend that the cards be kept in a special scarf (a silk scarf, if possible) and that they not be handled by anyone else. This is supposed to concentrate and sustain the energies of your cards. You will discover for yourself the proper way to handle the tarot cards.

It can be very helpful to conduct the tarot session as a serious ritual or a meditative exercise.

— Choose a quiet place and turn off radio, television, and telephone.
— Close your eyes and consciously relax for some minutes, letting the breath flow freely.
— Create a suitable atmosphere with candlelight and/or incense.
— Hold the cards for some moments in your hand and concentrate on the questions.
— Thoroughly shuffle the cards, possibly cut them, and lay them out with the left hand.

There are two ways of selecting the cards as you lay them out. You can take each card in sequence from the top of the deck, or you can fan out the cards into a half-circle and intuitively (with closed or opened eyes) pick with your left hand a card for every position of the spread.

Every ritualization involves the danger of becoming dogmatic. An exaggerated tarot ritual can also lead to taking the cards dead seriously—and thereby suppressing your own creativity. This is a question of balance—see card 14 Wholeness.

Every "answer" from the tarot system symbolically stands for the energy, emotional state, and dimension of consciousness in effect at the given moment. Every tarot answer is then a reflection of your own psychic pattern of life, not a verdict or judgment made by abstract, outer, authoritative powers or gods.

The insight and help offered by every answer through the tarot is an invitation to self-determination, to creatively shaping your life, to freedom!

If you are just learning to use the tarot, it may be best for you to start with only the cards of the Major Arcana. All of the spreads explained in the following section are effective with the cards of the Major Arcana.

The Major Arcana are completely adequate at first to touch upon associations, emotional reactions, memories, and deep insights.

If you are advanced, you may wish to add the court cards. If you are a tarot expert, you will probably often work with all of the cards and in certain situations intentionally use only the cards of the Major Arcana. If you have to look frequently at the instruction book in order to be clear on the possible meaning of the cards, we recommend that you just concentrate on the cards of the Major Arcana.

When using the complete deck keep the following in mind.

The cards of the Major Arcana are particularly meaningful for seeing transcendental energies, characteristics often not yet conscious, and the fundamental structure of one's personality or current life. They show inner, archetypal powers that determine our lives.

The personality or court cards stand for the traits and abilities which rule at the time, and have already been fulfilled or which are being expressed. They also show vividly experienced wishes of the self, and ego strategies which are striven for or are already in use.

The numbered cards indicate passing states of mind and moods or external influences of limited duration.

It is possible to combine the cards of the Tarot of Love with other decks. For example, in the Star of Love Spread, you can pull the individual "question card" (card 1) from the Tarot of Love, then draw cards from the other deck for the rest of the spread. You may wish to do a reading together with your partner, each one with his or her own spread. For this, two decks may be best, so that each partner has access to all the cards. You can also use one deck and take turns drawing cards: One partner draws a card for card 1 of his or her spread, then the other partner draws for card 1 of his or her spread, and so on. Of course, each spread can be done one at a time, with the first spread noted on paper before the cards are regathered and shuffled for the second spread.

The Arrow of Time

The Arrow of Time is a spread for a quick and concise survey or an instant insight; it is a simple method to assess the dynamics of time in an ongoing development.

Using three cards, the Arrow of Time focuses on the energies relevant to a certain situation in the past, the present, and the future.

Lay down the card for the past on the left, then draw the card for the present and lay it down in the middle. Finally, put the third card for the future on the right.

Card 1: The past. The characteristics, abilities, qualities, expectations, hopes, and wishes we have brought into the part-

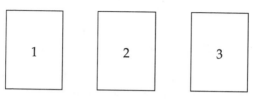

THE ARROW OF TIME

nership. The spiritual, mental, emotional, and/or material foundations on which the relationship has been built—from our point of view. Our own past, as it affects our life today.

If a card in this position is felt to be "negative," it points out fears that have not yet been made conscious, the suppressed "shadow," the powers that are hidden in the depths of our psyches and that seem to threaten us and the partnership. Alternately, if we are working with a tarot deck that has negative imagery, we may be taking the pictures on the cards literally instead of interpreting them symbolically.

Card 2: The present. The energy vibrations that currently affect the partnership. The challenges, tasks, problems, or opportunities that confront us. The main issues and themes in our relationship.

If a card in this position appears to be negative, it is likely that we refuse to confront difficulties and want to avoid them.

Card 3: The future. The aspirations, desires, and expectations that will define our partnership in the near future. The energies and dimensions of consciousness that will open up to us through the partnership. The potential for growth.

If a card in this position seems to have a negative reading, we should check to see if we are afraid that the future will remain uncertain or that our own negative projections will turn into reality.

The Star of Love

The Star of Love was designed especially for the Tarot of Love. The Star of Love enables us to gain clear insights into the most decisive causes and influences on human relationships and communications. This distinct technique has already proven itself in many tarot readings.

The Star of Love illustrates substantial forces guiding or even controlling the direction in which the topic in question is likely to develop. This tarot spread lends itself particularly well to the combined use of the Tarot of Love with cards of other decks.

Card 1. This card represents the issue at hand and occupies the center of the spread. Before the deck is shuffled, card 1 is selected according to the correspondences given in the list following this outline of the Star of Love. It is placed face up in position 1.

The next five cards are drawn after you have shuffled and cut the remaining cards.

Card 2. Feminine energies and influences affecting the question.

Card 3. Masculine energies and influences.

Card 4. Lessons from the past (or past lives, if we believe in reincarnation) which are still in effect.

Card 5. Our hopes, desires, intentions, and goals in respect to the question, ideally pointing toward the result or solution we want to achieve.

Card 6. Supportive or challenging forces, beneficial factors, or the nature of any obstacles to attaining our goal.

The Star of Love allows us to focus our energies on

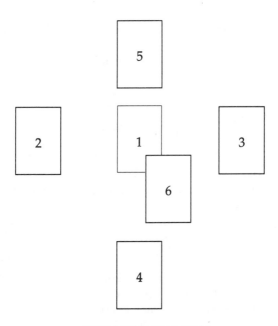

THE STAR OF LOVE

specific issues and particular questions with the laying out of a relevant card face up in the center of the spread (position 1). The following list of individual cards corresponding to specific topics will help you to find the right "catalyst" for an enhanced focus of energies.

Decision on a partner for love: 6 The Lovers. No further comment needed.

Decision on marriage: 7 Companionship. We need to be clear about the fact that any kind of commitment requires a minimum of closeness, agreement, and harmony in regard to the realization of intimacy, friendship, and common goals.

Decision between two love partners: 12 Reversal. If we cannot decide by employing usual means and methods to make up our minds, we need a completely new, fresh, and unique point of view.

Desire to have children: 19 The Sun, if a woman asks. 18 The Moon, if a man asks. The card that complements the person putting out this question generates necessary focus.

Sexual fulfillment: 6 The Lovers, if the question refers to a present passion or desire that does not pose a serious problem. 15 Entanglement, if we are dealing with a complicated situation in which one partner has desires not shared by the other. 11 Climax, if the question concerns sexual aspirations not yet experienced, not openly admitted, or seemingly out of reach.

Spiritual union: 17 The Star, showing us how cosmic energies stimulate the earth. The yearning for spiritual union is always nurtured by a fusion of human consciousness with energies from higher spheres.

Desire for better communication: 14 Wholeness. Real communication, real sharing, can be achieved only if and when we balance our creative energies and are at one with our soul.

Separation: 16 Lightning. This card symbolizes sudden breakups, unexpected "destruction," parting, dissolution, and disillusionment; it stands for the inevitability and necessity of change and thus it also stands for separation.

Divorce: 13 Transformation. What may be felt to be a form of "death" is in reality just one form of change. A single person moves from a dark existence into a colorful and uplifted new state of being. Take the time to look at how Marcia Perry has rendered this card; it radiates much comfort and encouragement.

Death of a partner: 0 The Fools. Someday each one of us will take leave of this planet and let go of our physical bodies to cross the tightrope of life toward a transcendent destiny. There is no "death" or separation on this plane of consciousness or in the realms of the soul. Soul energy will never be annihilated, it will be transformed. Every soul is and remains intertwined with others. The Fools inspire us to follow their example in cheerfully letting go of each other on the material plane, even in such difficult times.

Loneliness and being alone in a partnership: 9 The Seekers. To be alone (all-one) does not have to mean being lonely. People who lead a conscious life are aware of this. Each person in a relationship needs space once in a while, some time on their own, and must allow the partner to fulfill that need.

Soul mates, twin souls: 21 The World, or 22 Soul Mates. Depending on our personal way of relating better to one card or the other, either card serves to focus our vibration to that rare state of partnership on the level of the soul. Such a relationship supports self-realization by using spiritual insight under the most challenging conditions: those of an intimate partnership down here on this earth.

Other questions: 10 Destiny. The wheel of life with its unavoidable and unforeseeable ups and downs provides the background for all other issues.

You are always free to select the card that you feel is best suited for your individual question. In summary, you pick out the special card which most aptly fits your question and put it in the center of the spread, in position 1. Then shuffle the rest of deck while concentrating on your question and the energy of the central card. Draw five cards one after the other and lay them down in positions 2 through 6, as shown in the diagram.

The Tarot Partner Dialogue

Both partners shuffle the cards and both may want to cut them. Next, fan out the cards in a half circle in front of you. While concentrating on each question listed, you each draw a card. You may choose to keep your eyes closed while drawing. This manner of consciously and openly taking part in a tarot session supports the flow of energy, the intuitive ability to interpret, and the willingness for transformation.

The answer cards of the partners are laid down next to each other.

— What do I want from you?
   Card 1 drawn by one partner, card 2 by the other partner.
— What do I give you?
   Card 3 drawn by one partner, card 4 by the other partner.
— What bothers me about you?
   Card 5 drawn by one partner, card 6 by the other partner.
— What do I love about you?
   Card 7 drawn by one partner, card 8 by the other partner.
— Where do I want to go with you?
   Card 9 drawn by one partner, card 10 by the other partner.
— What do you want from me?
   Card 11 drawn by one partner, card 12 by the other partner.

The list of questions can be expanded or changed as you wish. Questions can also be turned around. Instead of asking, "What bothers me about you?" you can ask, "What bothers you about me?"

This simple and yet astonishingly vivid partner dialogue through tarot cards can increase spontaneous in-depth communication and reveal emotional blocks.

More possible questions:

— What do you represent for me? What do I represent for you?
— What do I expect from you? What do you expect from me?
— What do you change in me? What do I change in you?
— Which direction of growth do I see in our relationship? Which direction of growth do you see in our relationship?

TAROT PARTNER DIALOGUE

The Celtic Cross

The Celtic Cross is a traditional spread that we have modified to suit the Tarot of Love and its way of treating issues of love, relationships, friendships, and family.

Shuffle and cut the tarot deck as you would ordinarily do and then draw ten cards, one after the other. Lay them out according to the diagram.

Card 1. The current theme or issue in the relationship.

Card 2. Current supporting factors or challenges in dealing with this issue within the relationship.

Card 3. The potential for growth within the relationship and the potential mutual goals of the partners.

Card 4. Past emotional energies that are still effective karmic influences.

Card 5. Past material conditions that have an influence on the relationship.

Card 6. The dynamic outer structures that may shape the present relationship in the near future.

Card 7. Our personal attitude or opinion regarding the question.

Card 8. The attitude or opinion of our partner regarding the question.

Card 9. Future challenges and tests to the relationship.

Card 10. The "result" as suggested by the prevailing energies. This card may also show the qualities and characteristics of a new beginning within the partnership.

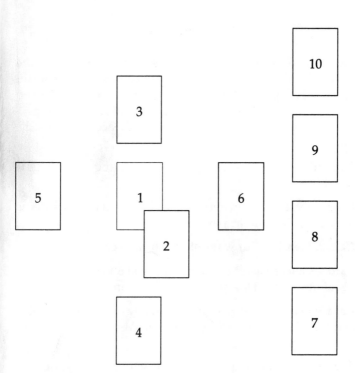

THE CELTIC CROSS

The Astro-Tarot

The Astro-Tarot spread transcribes the twelve signs of the zodiac and the twelve astrological houses into a tarot spread. The Astro-Tarot as used in the Tarot of Love interprets all twelve cards in reference to relationships.

Shuffle, cut, and lay out the cards according to the illustration.

Card 1: Aries. Our attitude toward the partner and the relationship.

Card 2: Taurus. Our material, financial expectations; patterns of behavior within the partnership.

Card 3: Gemini. Our ways of sharing and communicating.

Card 4: Cancer. Past experiences and often unconscious desires about our home. This can be an inner or an external home.

Card 5: Leo. Opportunities for creatively realizing happiness and life's joys within the partnership. Also, procreation and birth.

Card 6: Virgo. Hints about our tasks within the relationship, what is to be learned, and where we can serve. Also, health, nutrition, and a natural lifestyle.

Card 7: Libra. The attitudes we expect our partner to have toward us. Unfulfilled or misguided expectations always lead to disappointment and disillusionment.

Card 8: Scorpio. Crises and transformational changes which are due to unrealistic expectations concerning the relationship. Sometimes, this card denotes an inheritance from the partner's family.

Card 9: Sagittarius. Spiritual orientation and the discovery of new horizons and goals within a partnership.

Card 10: Capricorn. How we can solidify our relationship and make it count for common social concerns. Also, establishing mutual material gains.

Card 11: Aquarius. Opportunities, as well as fears that are still latent and will have to be lived out or resolved.

Card 12: Pisces. Individual development and the freedom to be gained by dealing consciously with the challenges of partnership. Card 12 indicates how we will no longer (mis)use the

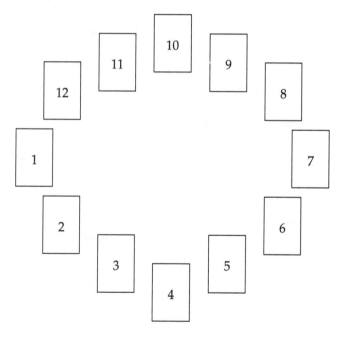

THE ASTRO-TAROT SPREAD

partner for our needs, fears, desires, or habits, but instead relate with creative self-determination. We can then continuously experience new encounters—even with the same partner. If we do not live consciously enough, we will constantly repeat the same old games—with the same partner or with changing partners. This card stands for the ideal flow of energy or the ultimate energy block. If its message is not clear enough, you may want to draw one more card for clarification.

In Closing

We have reached the end of this book. By now, you have picked up the tarot cards and spread them, played with them, read them, and reflected on them. . . .

Through the interpretations of the Tarot of Love you have probably not only received new impulses for dealing with the cards, but have also been spurred on to think about how you handle love, partnership, and interpersonal relationships in general.

We hope that we were able to share with you something of the happiness, joy of life, and inspiration which we and our partners, clients, and friends have felt time and again—in seminars, individual sessions, and naturally also in our own relationships—when we apply the Tarot of Love.

Essential in the Tarot of Love are openness, willingness to learn, and sympathy for other people and yourself. Be prepared to see all of life, including the complex, often complicated and challenging passionate partnerships, to be a great opportunity, the chance to experience new wonders every hour of every day, to give and to take, to work creatively on building a better world within a small scope and in a larger one as well—and to have fun doing it!

A word of thanks . . .

— to you for being interested in the Tarot of Love. With your interest, your positive thoughts, and your vibrations, you help in promoting life-affirming, constructive approaches to a conscious view of the world. If you use the Tarot of Love with this attitude, it will bring you much blessing and joy;

— to the many people who have helped us on our way to a positive view of life and who have helped us form the Tarot of Love. Our friends and teachers are too many to list by name—they will know that we talk about them;

and a heart-felt thank you

— to the staff members of Ariston Verlag who encouraged and helped us with much love, empathy, and trust; to the people at AG Mueller, who so heartily supported Marcia Perry's cards;

— to Stuart R. Kaplan, president of U.S. Games Systems, who enthusiastically undertook to publish the English-language edition;

— and to Jean Hoots, who edited and designed the English-language edition.

Thank you!

Suggested Reading

Griscom, Chris, and Wulfing von Rohr. *The Healing of Emotion*. New York: Fireside, Simon & Schuster, 1990.

Griscom, Chris, and Wulfing von Rohr. *Time Is an Illusion*. New York: Fireside, Simon & Schuster, 1989.

Kaplan, Stuart R. *The Encyclopedia of Tarot*. Volumes I, II, and III. Illustrations of tarot decks from all over the world, from the fifteenth century to the present, with commentary and historical background.

Mertz, Bernd A. *Astrology and Tarot*. Germany: Ansata Publishing. The relationship between the Major Arcana of the tarot and astrology.

Mertz, Bernd A. *Karma in Tarot*. Freiburg, Germany: Verlag Hermann Bauer, 1988. This gives us a look into the past instead of the future.

Nichols, Sallie. *Jung and Tarot*. York Beach, Maine: Samuel Weiser, 1982. Deals with the Major Arcana on the basis of C.G. Jung's psychology.

Waite, A. E. *The Pictorial Key to the Tarot*. Stamford, Conn.: U.S. Games Systems, 1982. Waite's own explanation of the Rider-Waite Tarot.

Ziegler, Gerd. *Tarot: Mirror of the Soul*. Sauerlach, Germany: Urania Verlag, 1986. Explanation of the Crowley Book of Thoth Tarot.